Python Continuous Integration and Delivery

A Concise Guide with Examples

Moritz Lenz

Apress®

Python Continuous Integration and Delivery: A Concise Guide with Examples

Moritz Lenz
Fürth, Bayern, Germany

ISBN-13 (pbk): 978-1-4842-4280-3   ISBN-13 (electronic): 978-1-4842-4281-0
https://doi.org/10.1007/978-1-4842-4281-0

Library of Congress Control Number: 2018967720

Managing Director, Apress Media LLC: Welmoed Spahr
Acquisitions Editor: Steve Anglin
Development Editor: Matthew Moodie
Coordinating Editor: Mark Powers

Cover designed by eStudioCalamar

Cover image designed by Freepik (www.freepik.com)

Distributed to the book trade worldwide by Springer Science+Business Media New York, 233 Spring Street, 6th Floor, New York, NY 10013. Phone 1-800-SPRINGER, fax (201) 348-4505, e-mail orders-ny@springer-sbm.com, or visit www.springeronline.com. Apress Media, LLC is a California LLC and the sole member (owner) is Springer Science+Business Media Finance Inc (SSBM Finance Inc). SSBM Finance Inc is a Delaware corporation.

For information on translations, please e-mail editorial@apress.com; for reprint, paperback, or audio rights, please e-mail bookpermissions@springernature.com.

Apress titles may be purchased in bulk for academic, corporate, or promotional use. eBook versions and licenses are also available for most titles. For more information, reference our Print and eBook Bulk Sales web page at www.apress.com/bulk-sales.

Any source code or other supplementary material referenced by the author in this book is available to readers on GitHub via the book's product page, located at www.apress.com/9781484242803. For more detailed information, please visit www.apress.com/source-code.

Printed on acid-free paper

Table of Contents

About the Author

Moritz Lenz is a prolific blogger, author, and contributor to Open Source projects.

He works as software architect and principal software engineer for a midsize IT outsourcing company, where he has created a Continuous Integration and Delivery system for over 50 software libraries and applications.

About the Technical Reviewer

 **Michael Thomas** has worked in software development for over 20 years as an individual contributor, team lead, program manager, and vice president of engineering. Michael has more than 10 years of experience working with mobile devices. His current focus is in the medical sector, using mobile devices to accelerate information transfer between patients and health-care providers.

Acknowledgments

Writing a book is not a solitary endeavor and is only possible with help from many individuals and organizations. I would like to thank all of my beta readers who provided feedback. These include, in no particular order, Karl Vogel, Mikhail Itkin, Carl Mäsak, Martin Thurn, Shlomi Fish, Richard Lippmann, Richard Foley, and Roman Filippov. Paul Cochrane deserves special thanks for reviewing and providing feedback on the blog posts and manuscript and for being available to discuss content, ideas, and organization matters.

I also want to thank my publishing team at Apress: Steve Anglin, Mark Powers, and Matthew Moodie, as well as everybody doing awesome work in the background, such as cover design, typesetting, and marketing.

Finally, thanks go to my parents, for kindling both my love for books and engineering. And most important, to my family: to Signe, my wife, for constant support; and to my daughters, Ida and Ronja, for keeping me grounded in the real world and bringing joy to my life.

Introduction

One of the keys to successful software development is getting fast feedback. This helps developers avoid going down blind alleys, and in the case of a bug that is revealed quickly, it can be fixed while the code is still fresh in the developer's mind.

On the business side, fast feedback also helps the stakeholders and the product manager not to build features that turn out not to be useful, thus avoiding wasted effort. Achieving a mutual understanding about the desired product is a very difficult problem in any software project. Showing a working (if partial) product early on often helps to eliminate misunderstandings between stakeholders and developers.

There are many ways to add feedback loops on different levels, from adding linting and other code checks in the IDE to agile processes that emphasize incremental value delivery. The first part of this book focuses on software tests and their automatic execution, a practice known as continuous integration (CI).

When implementing CI, you set up a server that automatically tests every change to the source code, potentially in multiple environments, such as on combinations of operating system and programming language versions.

The next logical step, and the topic of the second part of this book, is continuous delivery (CD). After building and testing code, you add more steps to the automated process: automated deployment to one or more test environments, more tests in the installed state, and, finally, deployment to a production environment. The last step is typically guarded by a manual approval gate.

CD extends the automation and, thus, the possibility for quick iteration cycles, all the way into the production environment, where the software can deliver value for you. With such a mechanism in place, you can quickly obtain feedback or usage data from real customers and assess whether expanding on a feature is useful or discover bugs while the developers still remember the code that they wrote.

The code examples in this book use Python. Owing to its dynamic nature, Python is well-suited to small experiments and fast feedback. The well-stocked standard library and vast ecosystem of available libraries and frameworks, as well as Python's clean syntax, make it a good choice, even for larger applications. Python is commonly used in many domains, for example, web development, data science and machine learning, Internet of things (IoT), and system automation. It is becoming the lingua franca of professional programmers and those who just touch a subject to automate some part of their job or hobby.

Python comes in two major language versions, 2 and 3. Because Python 2 support is scheduled to end in 2020, and nearly all major libraries now support Python 3, new projects should be started in Python 3, and legacy applications should be ported to that language version as well, if possible. Hence, this book assumes that "Python" refers to Python 3, unless explicitly stated otherwise. If you only know Python 2, rest assured that you will easily understand the source code contained in this book, and transferring the knowledge to Python 3 is very easy.

I. 1 Intended Audience

This book is targeted at technical people involved in the software-delivery process: software developers, architects, release engineers, and DevOps engineers.

The chapters that use source code examples assume basic familiarity with the Python programming language. If you are familiar with other programming languages, spending a few hours reading introductory material on Python will likely bring you to a level at which you can easily follow the code examples in this book.

The sample infrastructure uses Debian GNU/Linux, so familiarity with that operating system is helpful, though not required.

I. 2 Code Examples

Code examples used in this book are available on GitHub under the python-ci-cd organization at https://github.com/python-ci-cd or via the Download Source Code link located at www.apress.com/9781484242803.

Because some examples rely on automatically fetching code from certain Git repositories, a split into several repositories is necessary. Several chapters reference individual repositories under this namespace.

CHAPTER 1

Automated Testing

Before diving into examples of how to test Python code, the nature of tests must be discussed in more detail. Why do we want to have tests? What do we gain from them? What are the downsides? What makes a good test; what's a bad test? How can we classify tests? And how many of which kinds of tests should we write?

1.1 What Do We Want from a Test?

Why bother with writing tests at all? There are a number of reasons why we want to write or, at least, have tests.

It is not uncommon to have several tests in a test suite, written in response to different needs.

Fast Feedback

Every change to code comes with the risk of introducing bugs. Research shows that somewhere in the range of 7% to 20% of all bug fixes introduce new bugs.[1]

---

[1] Jim Bird, "Bugs and Numbers: How Many Bugs Do You Have in Your Code?" Building Real Software: Developing and Maintaining Secure and Reliable Software in the Real World, `http://swreflections.blogspot.de/2011/08/bugs-and-numbers-how-many-bugs-do-you.html`, August 23, 2011.

© Moritz Lenz 2019
M. Lenz, *Python Continuous Integration and Delivery*,
https://doi.org/10.1007/978-1-4842-4281-0_1

Wouldn't it be great if we could find those bugs before they find their way to the customer? Or even before your colleagues see them? This is not just a question of vanity. If you receive quick feedback that you have introduced a bug, you are more likely to remember all the details of the part of the code base you just worked on, so fixing the bug tends to be much faster when you get fast feedback.

Many test cases are written to give this kind of fast feedback loop. You can often run them before you ever commit your changes to the source control system, and they make your work more efficient and keep your source control history clear.

Confidence

Related to the previous point, but worth mentioning separately, is the confidence boost you can get from knowing that the test suite will catch simple mistakes for you. In most software-based businesses, there are critical areas where serious bugs could endanger the whole business. Just imagine you, as a developer, accidentally mess up the login system of a health-care data management product, and now people see others' diagnoses. Or imagine that automatic billing charges the wrong amount to customers' credit cards.

Even non-software businesses have had catastrophic failures from software errors. Both the Mars climate orbiter[2] and the first launch of the Ariane 5 rocket[3] suffered the loss of the respective vehicle, owing to software issues.

---

[2]Wikipedia, "Mars Climate Orbiter," https://en.wikipedia.org/wiki/Mars_Climate_Orbiter, 2018.

[3]J. L. Lions, "Ariane 5: Flight 501 Failure. Report by the Inquiry Board," http://sunnyday.mit.edu/accidents/Ariane5accidentreport.html, July 1996.

The criticality of their work puts emotional stress on software developers. Automated tests and good development methodology can help alleviate this stress.

Even if the software that people are developing is not mission-critical, risk adversity can cause developers or maintainers to make the smallest change possible and put off necessary refactoring that would keep the code maintainable. The confidence that a good test suite provides can enable developers to do what is necessary to keep the code base from becoming the proverbial big ball of mud.[4]

Debugging Aid

When developers change code, which in turn causes a test to fail, they want the test to be helpful in finding the bug. If a test simply says "something is wrong," this knowledge is better than not knowing about the bug. It would be even more helpful if the test could provide a hint to start debugging.

If, for example, a test failure indicates that the function `find_shortest_path` raised an exception, rather than returning a path, as expected, we know that either that function (or one it called) broke, or it received wrong input. That's a much better debugging aid.

Design Help

The Extreme Programming (XP)[5] movement advocates that you should practice *test-driven development* (TDD). That is, before you write any code that solves a problem, you first write a failing test. Then you write just enough code to pass the test. Either you are done, or you write the next test. Rinse and repeat.

---

[4]Wikipedia, "Big ball of mud," `https://en.wikipedia.org/wiki/Big_ball_of_mud`, 2018.

[5]Wikipedia, "Extreme programming," `https://en.wikipedia.org/wiki/Extreme_programming`, 2018.

This has obvious advantages: you make sure that all code you write has test coverage and that you don't write unnecessary or unreachable code. However, TDD practitioners have also reported that the test-first approach helped them write better code. One aspect is that writing a test forces you to think about the application programming interface (API) that the implementation will have, and so you start implementing with a better plan in mind. Another reason is that pure functions (functions whose return value depends only on the input and that don't produce side effects or read data from databases, etc.) are very simple to test. Thus, the test-first approach guides the developer toward a better separation of algorithms or business logic from supporting logic. This separation of concerns is an aspect of good software design.

It should be noted that not everybody agrees with these observations, with counterpoints from experience or arguments that some code is much harder to test than write, leading to a waste of effort, by requiring tests for everything. Still, the design help that tests can provide is a reason why developers write code and so should not be missing here.

Specification of the Product

The days of big, unified specification documents for software projects are mostly over. Most projects follow some iterative development model, and even if there is a detailed specification document, it is often outdated.

When there is no detailed and up-to-date prose specification, the test suite can take the role of specification. When people are unsure how a program should behave in a certain situation, a test might provide the answer. For programming languages, data formats, protocols, and other things, it might even make sense to offer a test suite that can be used for validating more than one implementation.

1.2 Downsides of Tests

It would be disingenuous to keep quiet about the downsides that tests can have. These downsides should not detract you from writing tests, but being aware of them will help you decide what to test, how to write the tests, and, maybe, how many tests to write.

Effort

It takes time and effort to write tests. So, when you are tasked with implementing a feature, you not only have to implement the feature but also write tests for it, resulting in more work and less time do other things that might provide direct benefit to the business. Unless, of course, the tests provide enough time savings (for example, through not having to fix bugs in the production environment and clean up data that was corrupted through a bug) to amortize the time spent on writing the tests.

Extra Code to Maintain

Tests are code themselves and must be maintained, just like the code that is being tested. In general, you want the least amount of code possible that solves your problem, because the less code you have, the less code must be maintained. Think of code (including test code) as a liability rather than an asset.

If you write tests along with your features and bug fixes, you have to change those tests when requirements change. Some of the tests also require changing when refactoring, making the code base harder to change.

Brittleness

Some tests can be brittle, that is, they occasionally give the wrong result. A test that fails even though the code in question is correct is called a *false positive*. Such a test failure takes time to debug, without providing any value. A *false negative* is a test that does not fail when the code under test is broken. A false negative test provides no value either but tends to be much harder to spot than false positives, because most tools draw attention to failed tests.

Brittle tests undermine the trust in the test suite. If deployment of a product with failing tests becomes the norm because everybody assumes those failed tests are false positives, the signaling value of the test suite has dropped to zero. You might still use it to track which of the tests failed in comparison to the last run, but this tends to degenerate into a lot of manual work that nobody wants to do.

Unfortunately, some kinds of tests are very hard to do robustly. Graphical user interface (GUI) tests tend to be very sensitive to layout or technology changes. Tests that rely on components outside your control can also be a source of brittleness.

False Sense of Security

A flawless run of a test suite can give you a false sense of security. This can be due either to false negatives (tests that should fail but do not) or missing test scenarios. Even if a test suite achieves 100% statement coverage of the tested code, it might miss some code paths or scenarios. Thus, you see a passing test run and take that as an indication that your software works correctly, only to be flooded with error reports once real customers get in contact with the product.

There is no direct solution for the overconfidence that a test suite can provide. Only through experience with a code base and its tests will you get a feeling for realistic confidence levels that a green (i.e., passing) test run provides.

1.3 Characteristics of a Good Test

A good test is one that combines several of the reasons for writing tests, while avoiding the downsides as much as possible. This means the test should be fast to run, simple to understand and maintain, give good and specific feedback when it fails, and be robust.

Maybe somewhat surprisingly, it should also fail occasionally, albeit when one expects the test to fail. A test that never fails also never gives you feedback and can't help you with debugging. That doesn't mean you should delete a test for which you never recorded a failure. Maybe it failed on a developer's machine, and he or she fixed the bug before checking changes.

Not all tests can fit all of the criteria for good tests, so let's look at some of the different kinds of tests and the trade-offs that are inherent to them.

1.4 Kinds of Tests

There is a traditional model of how to categorize tests, based on their scope (how much code they cover) and their purpose. This model divides code that tests for correctness into unit, integration, and system tests. It also adds smoke tests, performance tests, and others for different purposes.

Unit Tests

A unit test exercises—in isolation—the smallest unit of a program that makes sense to cover. In a procedural or functional programming language, that tends to be a subroutine or function. In an object-oriented language such as Python, it could be a method. Depending on how strictly you interpret the definition, it could also be a class or a module.

A unit test should avoid running code outside the tested unit. So, if you are testing a database-heavy business application, your unit test should still not perform calls to the database (access the network for API calls) or the file system. There are ways to substitute such external dependencies for testing purposes that I will discuss later, though if you can structure your code to avoid such calls, at least in most units, all the better.

Because access to external dependencies is what makes most code slow, unit tests are usually blazingly fast. This makes them a good fit for testing algorithms or core business logic.

For example, if your application is a navigation assistant, there is at least one algorithmically challenging piece of code in there: the router, which, given a map, a starting point, and a target, produces a route or, maybe, a list of possible routes, with metrics such as length and expected time of arrival attached. This router, or even parts of it, is something that you want to cover with unit tests as thoroughly as you can, including strange edge cases that might cause infinite loops, or check that a journey from Berlin to Munich doesn't send you via Rome.

The sheer volume of test cases that you want for such a unit makes other kinds of tests impractical. Also, you don't want such tests to fail, owing to unrelated components, so keeping them focused on a unit improves their specificity.

Integration Tests

If you assembled a complex system such as a car or a spacecraft from individual components, and each component works fine in isolation, what are the chances the thing as a whole works? There are so many ways things could go wrong: some wiring might be faulty, components want to talk through incompatible protocols, or maybe the joints can't withstand the vibration during operation.

It's no different in software, so one writes integration tests. An integration test exercises several units at once. This makes mismatches at the boundaries between units obvious (via test failures), enabling such mistakes to be corrected early.

System Tests

A system test puts a piece of software into an environment and tests it there. For a classical three-tiered architecture, a system test starts from input through the user interface and tests all layers down to the database.

Where unit tests and integration tests are white box tests (tests that require and make use of the knowledge of how the software is implemented), system tests tend to be black box tests. They take the user's perspective and don't care about the guts of the system.

This makes system tests the most realistic, in terms of how the software is put under test, but they come with several downsides.

First, managing dependencies for system tests can be really hard. For example, if you are testing a web application, you typically first need an account that you can use for login, and then each test case requires a fixed set of data it can work with.

Second, system tests often exercise so many components at once that a test failure doesn't give good clues as to what is actually wrong and requires that a developer look at each test failure, often to find out that changes are unrelated to the test failures.

Third, system tests expose failures in components that you did not intend to test. A system test might fail owing to a misconfigured Transport Layer Security (TLS) certificate in an API that the software uses, and that might be completely outside of your control.

Last, system tests are usually much slower than unit and integration tests. White box tests allow you to test just the components you want, so you can avoid running code that is not interesting. In a system test for a web application, you might have to perform a login, navigate to the page

9

that you want to test, enter some data, and then finally do the test you actually want to do. System tests often require much more setup than unit or integration tests, increasing their runtime and lengthening the time until one can receive feedback about the code.

Smoke Tests

A smoke test is similar to a system test, in that it tests each layer in your technology stack, though it is not a thorough test for each. It is usually not written to test the correctness of some part of your application but, rather, that the application works at all in its current context.

A smoke test for a web application could be as simple as a login, followed by a call to the user's profile page, verifying that the user's name appears somewhere on this page. This does not validate any logic but will detect things like a misconfigured web server or database server or invalid configuration files or credentials.

To get more out of a smoke test, you can add a status page or API end point to your application that performs additional checks, such as for the presence of all necessary tables in a database, the availability of dependent services, and so on. Only if all those runtime dependencies are met will the status be "OK," which a smoke test can easily determine. Typically, you write only one or two smoke tests for each deployable component but run them for each instance you deploy.

Performance Tests

The tests discussed so far focus on correctness, but nonfunctional qualities, such as performance and security, can be equally important. In principle, it is quite easy to run a performance test: record the current time, run a certain action, record the current time again. The difference between the two time recordings is the runtime of that action. If necessary, repeat and calculate some statistics (e.g., median, mean, standard deviation) from these values.

As usual, the devil is in the details. The main challenges are the creation of a realistic and reliable test environment, realistic test data, and realistic test scenarios.

Many business applications rely heavily on databases. So, your performance test environment also requires a database. Replicating a big production database instance for a testing environment can be quite expensive, both in terms of hardware and licensing costs. So, there is temptation to use a scaled-down testing database, which comes with the risk of invalidating the results. If something is slow in the performance tests, developers tend to say "that's just the weaker database; prod could handle that easily"—and they might be right. Or not. There is no way to know.

Another insidious aspect of environment setup is the many moving parts when it comes to performance. On a virtual machine (VM), you typically don't know how many CPU cycles the VM got from the hypervisor, or if the virtualization environment played funny tricks with the VM memory (such as swapping out part of the VM's memory to disk), causing unpredictable performance.

On physical machines (which underlie every VM as well), you run into modern power-management systems that control clock speed, based on thermal considerations, and in some cases, even based on the specific instructions used in the CPU.[6]

All of these factors lead to performance measurements being much more indeterministic than you might naively expect from such a deterministic system as a computer.

---

[6]Vlad Krasnov, "On the Dangers of Intel's Frequency Scaling," Cloudflare, https://blog.cloudflare.com/on-the-dangers-of-intels-frequency-scaling/, November 10, 2017.

1.5 Summary

As software developers, we want automated tests to give us fast feedback on changes, catch regressions before they reach the customer, and provide us enough confidence in a change that we can refactor code. A good test is fast, reliable, and has high diagnostic value when it fails.

Unit tests tend to be fast and have high diagnostic value but only cover small pieces of code. The more code a test covers, the slower and more brittle it tends to be become, and its diagnostic value decreases.

In the next chapter, we will look at how to write and run unit tests in Python. Then we will investigate how to run them automatically for each commit.

CHAPTER 2

Unit Testing in Python

Many programmers manually test the code they are writing by calling the piece of code they are developing, printing the result to the console, and visually scanning the output for correctness. This works for simple tasks but suffers from some problems:

- When the output gets large, it becomes harder to spot errors.

- When the programmer tires, it is easy to miss subtly incorrect output.

- When the implemented feature becomes larger, one tends to miss regressions in parts that were "tested" earlier.

- Because the informal test scripts are generally only useful for the programmer who wrote them, their utility is lost to other developers.

Thus, *unit testing* was invented, in which one writes sample calls to pieces of code and compares the return value to the expected value.

This comparison is typically done in a way that produces little or no output when the test passes and very obvious output otherwise. A *test harness* can be used to run tests from several test scripts and only report the errors and a statistical summary of the passed tests.

© Moritz Lenz 2019
M. Lenz, *Python Continuous Integration and Delivery*,
https://doi.org/10.1007/978-1-4842-4281-0_2

2.1 Digression: Virtualenvs

To run the unit tests we are going to write, we require some additional tools that are available as Python packages. To install them, you should use a tool called a *virtualenv*. This is a Python directory that contains a Python interpreter, package management programs such as pip, as well as symbolic links to the base Python packages, thus giving you a pristine Python environment on which to build a customized, isolated virtual environment containing exactly the libraries you need. A virtualenv enables you to install any Python package you want; you don't need root privileges in order to install a dependency for your application. You can activate one virtualenv within a given shell session and simply delete the directory when you don't need it anymore.

Virtualenvs are used to isolate separate development environments from each other and from the system Python installation. To create one, you need the virtualenv tool, which typically comes with your Python installation or, on Linux distributions, can be installed through the package manager. On Debian-based systems, you can install it like so:

```
$ sudo apt-get install virtualenv
```

To create a virtualenv called venv, run

```
$ virtualenv -p python3 venv
```

This prepares a directory called venv with the necessary files. Your next step should be to activate it, as follows:

```
$ source venv/bin/activate
```

Once you have activated it, you can install packages into it, using pip, e.g.:

```
$ pip install pytest
```

When you are done, disable it with the command deactivate.

2.2 Getting Started with Unit Tests

To illustrate unit testing, let's start with a single function and how to test it. The function I want to implement here is a *binary search*. Given a sorted list of numbers (we call it the haystack), search for another number (the needle) in it. If it's present, return the index at which it was found. If not, raise an exception of type ValueError. You can find the code and tests for this example at https://github.com/python-ci-cd/binary-search.

We start by looking at the middle element of the haystack. If it happens to be equal to the needle, we are done. If it is smaller than the needle, we can repeat the search in the left half of the haystack. If it's larger, we can continue the search in the right half of the haystack.

To keep track of the area inside the haystack that we need to search, we keep two indices, left and right, and in each iteration, move one of them closer to the other, cutting the space to be searched in half in each step.

This is what the first attempt at implementing this function looks like:

```python
def search(needle, haystack):
    left = 0
    right = len(haystack) - 1

    while left <= right:
        middle = left + (right - left) // 2
        middle_element = haystack[middle]
        if middle_element == needle:
            return middle
        elif middle_element < needle:
            left = middle
        else:
            right = middle
    raise ValueError("Value not in haystack")
```

The First Test

Does it work? Who knows? Let's find out by writing a test.

```python
def test_search():
    assert search(2, [1, 2, 3, 4]) == 1, \
        'found needle somewhere in the haystack'
```

This is a simple function that exercises the search function with sample inputs and uses assert to raise an exception if the expectation was not met. Instead of calling this test function directly, we use pytest, a command-line tool supplied by a Python package of the same name. If it is not available in your development environment, you can install it with the following command (remember to run it inside a virtualenv):

```
pip install pytest
```

When pytest is available, you can run it on the file containing both the search function and the test function, as follows:

```
$ pytest binary-search.py
==================== test session starts =====================
platform linux -- Python 3.5.2, pytest-3.3.2, py-1.5.2
rootdir: /home/moritz/examples, inifile:
collected 1 item

binary-search.py .                                   [100%]

================== 1 passed in 0.01 seconds ==================
```

The test run prints various pieces of information: These include details about the platform and version of the software involved, the working directory, and what pytest configuration file was used (none in this example).

The line `collected 1 item` then shows that `pytest` found one test function. The dot behind the file name in the next line shows the progress, with one dot for each test that has been executed.

In a terminal, the last line is shown in green, to indicate a passed test run. If we made a mistake, say, used 0 instead of 1, as the expected result, we'd get some diagnostic output, like the following:

```
=========================== FAILURES ===========================
_____test_search_____

        def test_search():
>           assert search(2, [1, 2, 3, 4]) == 0, \
                'found needle somewhere in the haystack'
E           AssertionError: found needle somewhere in the haystack
E           assert 1 == 0
E            + where 1 = search(2, [1, 2, 3, 4])

binary-search.py:17: AssertionError
================== 1 failed in 0.03 seconds ==================
```

This shows the test function that fails, both as source code and with values substituted in on both sides of the == operator in the `assert` call, showing exactly what went wrong. In a terminal with color support, the failed test and the status line at the bottom are shown in red, to make failed tests obvious.

Writing More Tests

Many bugs in code manifest themselves in edge cases, with empty lists or strings as inputs, numbers being zero, accessing the first and last element of lists, and so on. It is a good idea to think of these cases when writing tests and cover them. Let's start with searching for the first and the last element.

```python
def test_search_first_element():
    assert search(1, [1, 2, 3, 4]) == 0, \
        'search first element'

def test_search_last_element():
    assert search(4, [1, 2, 3, 4]) == 3, \
        'search last element'
```

The test for finding the first element passes, but the test for the last element hangs, that is, it runs indefinitely without terminating. You can abort the Python process by pressing the Ctrl and C keys simultaneously.

If function search can find the first but not the last element, there must be some kind of asymmetry in it. Indeed there is: determining the middle element uses the integer division operator //, which rounds positive numbers toward zero. For example, 1 // 2 == 0. This explains why the loop can get stuck: when right is equal to left + 1, the code sets middle to the value of left. If the branch left = middle is executed, the area of the haystack in which the function searches does not decrease in size, and the loop gets stuck.

There is an easy fix. Because the code has already determined that the element at index middle is not the needle, it can be excluded from the search.

```python
def search(needle, haystack):
    left = 0
    right = len(haystack) - 1

    while left <= right:
        middle = left + (right - left) // 2
        middle_element = haystack[middle]
        if middle_element == needle:
            return middle
        elif middle_element < needle:
            left = middle + 1
```

```
    else:
            right = middle - 1
raise ValueError("Value not in haystack")
```

With this fix in place, all three tests pass.

Testing the Unhappy Path

The tests so far focused on the "happy path," the path in which an element was found and no error encountered. Because exceptions are not the exception (excuse the pun) in normal control flow, they should be tested too.

pytest has some tooling that helps you verify that an exception is raised by a piece of code and that it is of the correct type.

```
def test_exception_not_found():
    from pytest import raises

    with raises(ValueError):
        search(-1, [1, 2, 3, 4])

    with raises(ValueError):
        search(5, [1, 2, 3, 4])

    with raises(ValueError):
        search(2, [1, 3, 4])
```

Here, we test three scenarios: that a value was smaller than the first element in the haystack, larger than the last, and, finally, that it is between the first and the last element in size but simply not inside the haystack.

The pytest.raises routine returns a *context manager*. Context managers are, among other things, a neat way to wrap code (inside the with ... block) in some other code. In this case, the context manager catches the exception from the with block, and the test passes if it is of the right type. Conversely, the test fails if either no exception was raised or one of a wrong type, such as a KeyError, was.

As with the assert statements before, you can give the tests labels. These are useful both for debugging test failures and for documenting the tests. With the raises function, you can pass in the test label as a named argument called message.

```
def test_exception_not_found():
    from pytest import raises

    with raises(ValueError, message="left out of bounds"):
        search(-1, [1, 2, 3, 4])

    with raises(ValueError, message="right out of bounds"):
        search(5, [1, 2, 3, 4])

    with raises(ValueError, message="not found in middle"):
        search(2, [1, 3, 4])
```

2.3 Dealing with Dependencies

Not all code is as simple to test, as with the search function from the previous sections. Some functions call external libraries or interact with databases, APIs, or the Internet.

In unit tests, you should avoid doing those external actions, for several reasons.

- The actions might have unwanted side effects, such as sending e-mails to customers or colleagues and confusing them or even causing harm.

- You typically do not have control over external services, which means you do not have control over consistent responses, which makes writing reliable tests much harder.

- Performing external actions, such as writing or deleting files, leaves the environment in a different state, which potentially leads to test results that cannot be reproduced.

- Performance suffers, which negatively impacts the development feedback cycle.

- Often, external services, such as databases or APIs, require credentials, which are a hassle to manage and pose a serious barrier to setting up a development environment and running tests.

How do you, then, avoid these external dependencies in your unit tests? Let's explore some options.

Separating Logic from External Dependencies

Many applications get data from somewhere, often different sources, then do some logic with it, and maybe print out the result in the end.

Let's consider the example of the application that counts keywords in a web site. The code for this could be the following (which uses the requests library; you can install it with pip install requests in your virtualenv):

```python
import requests

def most_common_word_in_web_page(words, url):
    """

    finds the most common word from a list of words
    in a web page, identified by its URL
    """

    response = requests.get(url)
    text = response.text
    word_frequency = {w: text.count(w) for w in words}
    return sorted(words, key=word_frequency.get)[-1]
```

```python
if __name__ == '__main__':
    most_common = most_common_word_in_web_page(
        ['python', 'Python', 'programming'],
        'https://python.org/',
    )
    print(most_common)
```

At the time of writing, this code prints Python as the answer, though this might change in future, at the discretion of the python.org maintainers.

You can find the sample code and tests at https://github.com/python-ci-cd/python-webcount.

This code uses the requests library to fetch the contents of a web page and accesses the resulting text (which is really HTML). The function then iterates over the search words, counts how often each occurs in the text (using the string.count method), and constructs a dictionary with these counts. It then sorts the lists of words by their frequency and returns the most commonly occurring one, which is the last element of the sorted list.

Testing most_common_word_in_web_page becomes tedious, owing to its use of the HTTP client requests. The first thing we can do is to split off the logic of counting and sorting from the mechanics of fetching a web site. Not only does this make the logic part easier to test, it also improves the quality of the code, by separating things that don't really belong together, thus increasing cohesion.

```python
import requests

def most_common_word_in_web_page(words, url):
    """

    finds the most common word from a list of words
    in a web page, identified by its URL
    """
```

```python
    response = requests.get(url)
    return most_common_word(words, response.text)

def most_common_word(words, text):
    """

    finds the most common word from a list of words
    in a piece of text
    """

    word_frequency = {w: text.count(w) for w in words}
    return sorted(words, key=word_frequency.get)[-1]

if __name__ == '__main__':
    most_common = most_common_word_in_web_page(
        ['python', 'Python', 'programming'],
        'https://python.org/',
    )
    print(most_common)
```

The function that does the logic, most_common_word, is now a *pure* function, that is, the return value only depends on the arguments passed to it, and it doesn't have any interactions with the outside world. Such a pure function is easy enough to test (again, tests go into test/functions.py).

```python
def test_most_common_word():
    assert most_common_word(['a', 'b', 'c'], 'abbbcc') \
            == 'b', 'most_common_word with unique answer'

def test_most_common_word_empty_candidate():
    from pytest import raises
    with raises(Exception, message="empty word raises"):
        most_common_word([], 'abc')

def test_most_common_ambiguous_result():
    assert most_common_word(['a', 'b', 'c'], 'ab') \
        in ('a', 'b'), "there might be a tie"
```

These tests are more examples for unit testing, and they also raise some points that might not have been obvious from simply reading the function's source code.

- `most_common_word` does not actually look for word boundaries, so it will happily count the "word" b three times in the string abbbcc.

- The function will raise an exception when called with an empty list of keywords, but we haven't bothered to specify what kind of error.[1]

- We haven't specified which value to return if two or more words have the same occurrence count, hence the last test using in with a list of two valid answers.

Depending on your situation, you might want to leave such tests as documentation of known edge cases or refine both the specification and the implementation.

Returning to the topic of testing functions with external dependencies, we have reached partial success. The interesting logic is now a separate, pure function and can be tested easily. The original function, most_common_word_in_web_page, is now simpler but still untested.

We have, implicitly, established the principle that it is acceptable to change code to make it easier to test, but it is worth mentioning explicitly. We will use it more in the future.

Dependency Injection for Testing

If we think more about what makes the function most_common_word_in_web_page hard to test, we can come to the conclusion that it's not just the interaction with the outside world through the HTTP user agent requests

---

[1] It actually raises an IndexError, from trying to access the last element of the sorted list, which is empty.

but also the use of the global symbol `requests`. If we made it possible to substitute it for another class, it would be easier to test. We can achieve this through a simple change to the function under test. (Comments have been stripped from the example for brevity.)

```python
def most_common_word_in_web_page(words, url,
        user_agent=requests):
    response = user_agent.get(url)
    return most_common_word(words, response.text)
```

Instead of using `requests` directly, the function now accepts an optional argument, `user_agent`, which defaults to `requests`. Inside the function, the sole use of `requests` has been replaced by `user_agent`.

For the caller, who calls the function with just two arguments, nothing changed. But the developer who writes the tests can now supply his/her own *test double*, a substitute implementation for a user agent that behaves in a deterministic way.

```python
def test_with_test_double():
    class TestResponse():
        text = 'aa bbb c'

    class TestUserAgent():
        def get(self, url):
            return TestResponse()

    result = most_common_word_in_web_page(
        ['a', 'b', 'c'],
        'https://python.org/',
        user_agent=TestUserAgent()
    )
    assert result == 'b', \
        'most_common_word_in_web_page tested with test double'
```

25

This test mimics just the parts of the `requests` API that the tested function uses. It ignores the `url` argument to the get method, so purely from this test, we can't be sure that the tested function uses the user agent class correctly. We could extend the test double to record the value of the argument that was passed in and check it later.

```python
def test_with_test_double():
    class TestResponse():
        text = 'aa bbb c'

    class TestUserAgent():
        def get(self, url):
            self.url = url
            return TestResponse()

    test_ua = TestUserAgent()
    result = most_common_word_in_web_page(
        ['a', 'b', 'c'],
        'https://python.org/',
        user_agent=test_ua
    )
    assert result == 'b', \
        'most_common_word_in_web_page tested with test double'
    assert test_ua.url == 'https://python.org/'
```

The technique demonstrated in this section is a simple form of *dependency injection*.[2] The caller has the option to inject an object or class on which a function depends.

Dependency injection is useful not just for testing but also for making software more pluggable. For example, you might want your software to be able to use different storage engines in different contexts, or different XML

---

[2]Wikipedia, "Dependency injection,"
https://en.wikipedia.org/wiki/Dependency_injection, 2018.

parsers, or any number of other pieces of software infrastructure for which multiple implementations exist.

Mock Objects

Writing test double classes can become tedious pretty quickly, because you often require one class per method called in the test, and all of these classes must be set up to correctly chain their responses. If you write multiple test scenarios, you either have to make the test doubles generic enough to cover several scenarios or repeat nearly the same code all over again.

Mock objects offer a more convenient solution. These are objects that you can easily configure to respond in predefined ways.

```python
def test_with_test_mock():
    from unittest.mock import Mock
    mock_requests = Mock()
    mock_requests.get.return_value.text = 'aa bbb c'
    result = most_common_word_in_web_page(
        ['a', 'b', 'c'],
        'https://python.org/',
        user_agent=mock_requests
    )
    assert result == 'b', \
        'most_common_word_in_web_page tested with test double'
    assert mock_requests.get.call_count == 1
    assert mock_requests.get.call_args[0][0] \
            == 'https://python.org/', 'called with right URL'
```

The first two lines of this test function import the class Mock and create an instance from it. Then the real magic happens.

```python
mock_requests.get.return_value.text = 'aa bbb c'
```

This installs an attribute, `get`, in object `mock_requests`, which, when it is called, returns another mock object. The attribute `text` on that second mock object has an attribute `text`, which holds the string `'aa bb c'`.

Let's start with some simpler examples. If you have a `Mock` object `m`, then `m.a = 1` installs an attribute `a` with value 1. On the other hand, `m.b.return_value = 2` configures `m`, so that `m.b()` returns 2.

You can continue to chain, so `m.c.return_value.d.e.return_value = 3` makes `m.c().d.e()` return 3. In essence, each `return_value` in the assignment corresponds to a pair of parentheses in the call chain.

In addition to setting up these prepared return values, mock objects also record calls. The previous example checked the `call_count` of a mock object, which simply records how often that mock has been called as a function.

The `call_args` property contains a tuple of arguments passed to its last call. The first element of this tuple is a list of positional arguments, the second a dict of named arguments.

If you want to check multiple invocations of a mock object, `call_args_list` contains a list of such tuples.

The `Mock` class has more useful methods. Please refer to the official documentation[3] for a comprehensive list.

Patching

Sometimes, dependency injection is not practical, or you don't want to risk changing existing code to get it under test. Then, you can exploit the dynamic nature of Python to temporarily override symbols in the tested code and replace them with test doubles—typically, mock objects.

---

[3]Python Software Foundation, "unittest.mock—mock object library,"
`https://docs.python.org/3/library/unittest.mock.html`, 2018.

```
from unittest.mock import Mock, patch

def test_with_patch():
    mock_requests = Mock()
    mock_requests.get.return_value.text = 'aa bbb c'
    with patch('webcount.functions.requests', mock_requests):
        result = most_common_word_in_web_page(
            ['a', 'b', 'c'],
            'https://python.org/',
        )
    assert result == 'b', \
        'most_common_word_in_web_page tested with test double'
    assert mock_requests.get.call_count == 1
    assert mock_requests.get.call_args[0][0] \
            == 'https://python.org/', 'called with right URL'
```

The call to the patch function (imported from unittest.mock, a standard library shipped with Python) specifies both the symbol to be patched (temporarily replaced) and the test double by which it is replaced. The patch function returns a context manager. So, after execution leaves the with block that the call occurs in, the temporary replacement is undone automatically.

When patching an imported symbol, it is important to patch the symbol in the namespace that it was imported in, not in the source library. In our example, we patched webcount.functions.requests, not requests.get.

Patching removes interactions with other code, typically libraries. This is good for testing code in isolation, but it also means that patched tests cannot detect misuse of libraries that have been patched out. Thus, it is important to write broader scoped tests, such as integration tests or acceptance tests, to cover correct usage of such libraries.

2.4 Separating Code and Tests

So far, we've put code and tests into the same file, just for the sake of convenience. However, code and tests serve different purposes, so as they grow in size, it is common to split them into different files and, typically, even into different directories. Our test code now also loads a module on its own (pytest), a burden that you don't want to put on production code. Finally, some testing tools assume different files for test and code, so we will follow this convention.

When developing a Python application, you typically have a package name for the project and a top-level directory of the same name. Tests go into a second top-level directory called tests. For example, the Django web framework has the directories django and test, as well as a README.rst as the entry point for beginners, and setup.py for installing the project.

Each directory that serves as a Python module must contain a file called __init__.py, which can be empty or contain some code. Typically, this code just imports other symbols, so that users of the module can import them from the top-level module name.

Let's consider a small application that, given a URL and a list of keywords, prints which of these keywords appears most often on web pages that the URL points to. We might call it webcount and put the logic into the file webcount/functions.py. Then, the file webcount/ __init__ .py would look like this:

```
from .functions import most_common_word_in_web_page
```

In each test file, we explicitly import the functions that we test, for instance:

```
from webcount import most_common_word_in_web_page
```

We can put test functions into any file in the test/ directory. In this instance, we put them into the file test/test_functions.py, to mirror the location of the implementation. The test_ prefix tells pytest that this is a file that contains tests.

Tweaking the Python Path

When you run this test with pytest test/test_functions.py, you will likely get an error like this:

```
test/functions.py:3: in <module>
    from webcount import most_common_word_in_web_page
E   ImportError: No module named 'webcount'
```

Python cannot find the module under test, webcount, because it is not located in Python's default module loading path.

You can fix this by adding the absolute path of your project's root directory to a file with the extension .pth into your virtualenv's site-packages directory. For example, if you use Python 3.5, and your virtualenv is in the directory venv/, you could put the absolute path into the file venv/lib/python3.5/site-packages/webcount.pth. Other methods of manipulating the "Python path" are discussed in the official Python documentation.[4]

A pytest-specific approach is to add an empty file, conftest.py, to your project's root directory. Pytest looks for files of that name and, on detecting their presence, marks the containing directory as a project to be tested and adds the directory to the Python path during the test run.

You don't have to specify the test file when invoking pytest. If you leave it out, pytest searches for all test files and runs them. The pytest documentation on integration practices[5] has more information on how this search works.

---

[4]https://docs.python.org/3/install/index.html#inst-search-path.
[5]https://docs.pytest.org/en/latest/goodpractices.html.

2.5 More on Unit Testing and Pytest

There are many more topics that you might encounter while trying to write tests for your code. For example, you might have to manage *fixtures*, pieces of data that serve as the baseline of your tests. Or you may have to patch functions from code that is loaded at runtime or do a number of other things that nobody prepared you for.

For such cases, the pytest documentation[6] is a good starting point. If you want a more thorough introduction, the book *Python Testing with pytest* by Brian Okken (The Pragmatic Bookshelf, 2017) is worth reading.

2.6 Running Unit Tests in Fresh Environments

Developers typically have a development environment in which they implement their changes, run the automatic and sometimes manual tests, commit their changes, and push them to a central repository. Such a development environment tends to accumulate Python packages that are not explicit dependencies of the software under development, and they tend to use just one Python version. These two factors also tend to make test suites not quite reproducible, which can lead to a "works on my machine" mentality.

To avoid that, you need a mechanism to easily execute a test suite in a reproducible manner and on several Python versions. The tox automation project[7] provides a solution: you supply it with a short configuration file, `tox.ini`, that lists Python versions and a standard `setup.py` file for installing the module. Then, you can just run the `tox` command.

---

[6]Pytest, "pytest: helps you write better programs," `https://docs.pytest.org/en/ latest/`, 2018.

[7]tox, "Welcome to the tox Automation Project," `https://tox.readthedocs.io/en/ latest/`, 2018.

The tox command creates a new virtualenv for each Python version, runs the tests in each environment, and reports the test status. First, we need a file setup.py.

```
# file setup.py
from setuptools import setup

setup(
    name = "webcount",
    version = "0.1",
    license = "BSD",
    packages=['webcount', 'test'],
    install_requires=['requests'],
)
```

This uses Python's library setuptools to make the code under development installable. Usually, you'd include more metadata, such as author, e-mail address, a more verbose description, etc.

Then, the file tox.ini tells tox how to run the tests, and in which environments.

```
[tox]
envlist = py35

[testenv]
deps = pytest
       requests
commands = pytest
```

The envlist in this example contains just py35 for Python 3.5. If you also want to run the tests on Python 3.6, you could write envlist = py35, py36. The key pypy35 would refer to the alternative *pypy* implementation of Python in version 3.5.

Now, calling tox runs the tests in all environments (here, just one), and at the end, reports on the status.

```
py35 runtests: PYTHONHASHSEED='3580365323'
py35 runtests: commands[0] | pytest
=================== test session starts ===================
platform linux -- Python 3.5.2, pytest-3.6.3, py-1.5.4,
    pluggy-0.6.0
rootdir: /home/[...]/02-webcount-patched, inifile:
collected 1 item

test/test_functions.py .                         [100%]

=============== 1 passed in 0.08 seconds ===============
_____summary_____

py35: commands succeeded
congratulations :)
```

2.7 Another Sample Project: matheval

Many projects these days are implemented as web services, so they can be used through HTTP—either as an API or through an actual web site. Let's consider a tiny web service that evaluates mathematical expressions that are encoded as trees in a JSON data structure. (You can find the full source code for this project at https://github.com/python-ci-cd/python-matheval/.) As an example, the expression 5 * (4 - 2) would be encoded as the JSON tree ["*", 5, ["+", 4, 2]] and evaluate to 10.

Application Logic

The actual evaluation logic is quite compact (see Listing 2-1).

Listing 2-1. File matheval/evaluator.py: Evaluation Logic

```python
from functools import reduce
import operator

ops = {
    '+': operator.add,
    '-': operator.add,
    '*': operator.mul,
    '/': operator.truediv,
}

def math_eval(tree):
    if not isinstance(tree, list):
        return tree
    op = ops[tree.pop(0)]
    return reduce(op, map(math_eval, tree))
```

Exposing it to the Web isn't much effort either, using the Flask framework (see Listing 2-2).

Listing 2-2. File matheval/frontend.py: Web Service Binding

```python
#!/usr/bin/python3

from flask import Flask, request

from matheval.evaluator import math_eval

app = Flask(__name__)

@app.route('/', methods=['GET', 'POST'])
def index():
    tree = request.get_json(force=True)
    result = math_eval(tree);
    return str(result) + "\n"

if __name__ == '__main__':
    app.run(debug=True)
```

Once you have added the project's root directory to a .pth file of your current virtualenv and installed the flask prerequisite, you can start a development server, like this:

```
$ python matheval/frontend.py
 * Serving Flask app "frontend" (lazy loading)
 * Environment: production
   WARNING: Do not use the development server in a production
   environment.
   Use a production WSGI server instead.
 * Debug mode: on
 * Running on http://127.0.0.1:5000/ (Press CTRL+C to quit)
```

For production usage, it is better to install gunicorn and then start the application as

```
$ gunicorn matheval.frontend:app
```

Unit testing the application logic is pretty straightforward, because it is a pure function (see Listing 2-3).

Listing 2-3. File test/test_evaluator.py: Unit Tests for Evaluating Expression Trees

```python
from matheval.evaluator import math_eval

def test_identity():
    assert math_eval(5) == 5, 'identity'

def test_single_element():
    assert math_eval(['+', 5]) == 5, 'single element'

def test_addition():
    assert math_eval(['+', 5, 7]) == 12, 'adding two numbers'

def test_nested():
    assert math_eval(['*', ['+', 5, 4], 2]) == 18
```

The index route is not complicated enough to warrant a unit test on its own, but in a later chapter, we will write a smoke test that exercises it once the application is installed.

We need a small setup.py file to be able to run the tests through pytest (see Listing 2-4).

Listing 2-4. File setup.py for matheval

```python
#!/usr/bin/env python

from setuptools import setup

setup(name='matheval',
      version='0.1',
      description='Evaluation of expression trees',
      author='Moritz Lenz',
      author_email='moritz.lenz@gmail.com',
      url='https://deploybook.com/',
      requires=['flask', 'pytest', 'gunicorn'],
      setup_requires=['pytest-runner'],
      packages=['matheval']
    )
```

Finally, we need an empty file conftest.py again and can now run the test.

```
$ pytest
===================== test session starts =====================
platform linux -- Python 3.6.5, pytest-3.8.0, py-1.6.0
rootdir: /home/moritz/src/matheval, inifile:
collected 4 items

test/test_evaluator.py ....                            [100%]

================== 4 passed in 0.02 seconds ==================
```

2.8 Summary

Unit tests exercise a piece of code in isolation, by calling it with sample inputs and verifying that it returns the expected result or throws the expected exception. With pytest, a test is a function whose name starts with `test_` and contains `assert` statements that verify return values. You run these test files with `pytest path/to/file.py`, and it finds and runs the tests for you. It makes test failures very obvious and tries to provide as much context as possible to debug them.

Mock objects provide a quick way to create test doubles, and the patching mechanism provides a convenient way to inject them into the tested code.

The `tox` command and project create isolated test environments that make test suites reproducible and more convenient to test on multiple Python versions and implementations.

CHAPTER 3

Continuous Integration with Jenkins

Once you have automated tests for your software, you must take care to keep those tests passing. With changes to the code or to infrastructure, or with new library versions, tests can start failing.

If you let them fail and don't do anything against this creeping entropy, the diagnostic value of the tests starts to drop, and new regressions tend to be covered up by the general noise. Keeping your tests passing, and continuously checking in new features and bug fixes, is a practice that must be part of the engineering culture of a software development team.

There are tools that can help the team. *Continuous integration* (CI) *servers* monitor version control repository and automatically run test suites on each new commit, possibly on a wide variety of platforms. They can notify developers when they've caused some tests to fail, give an overview of the history of a test job, and visualize trend data, such as test coverage.

When you use such a tool, it helps you to discover when tests start to fail, triage the failure to certain commits or platforms, and render the "it works on my machine" mantra obsolete, by providing an independent assessment. The engineers working on the software, however, still require the discipline to fix the test failures that a CI tool discovers.

© Moritz Lenz 2019
M. Lenz, *Python Continuous Integration and Delivery*,
https://doi.org/10.1007/978-1-4842-4281-0_3

3.1 Continuous Integration Servers

There are two kinds of CI servers, based on their deployment model. You install and run *on-premise* software on your own infrastructure, while cloud-based or *software as a service* (SaaS) software is typically run by the vendor that creates the CI server.

In enterprise settings, on-premise software tends to be the preferred solution, because it means the source code that is being tested doesn't have to leave the organization's network.

The most popular open source, on-premise CI server software is Jenkins,[1] a Java-based project under the MIT license, which we will use later in this chapter. Other examples in this category include Buildbot[2] (written in Python) and CruiseControl.[3] Popular closed source, on-premise CI software includes TeamCity[4] by JetBrains and Atlassian's Bamboo.[5]

In the realm of hosted CI services, Travis CI[6] is very popular, owing to its excellent integration with GitHub. Travis is also open source and can be self-hosted. AppVeyor[7] is frequently used for Windows-based CI. Both Travis and AppVeyor offer free plans for open source projects.

Most CI software has a central server component that can poll source code repositories for changes and that can also be triggered by hooks. If a change in the source code repository is detected, this triggers a job. The job can either be configured centrally in the server or in the source code repository. For example, Travis expects a file called `.travis.yml`, in the root of the repository that instructs Travis on how to prepare the environment and which commands to execute, to trigger the build and test.

---

[1]`https://jenkins.io/`.

[2]`http://buildbot.net/`.

[3]`http://cruisecontrol.sourceforge.net/`.

[4]`www.jetbrains.com/teamcity/`.

[5]`www.atlassian.com/software/bamboo`.

[6]`https://travis-ci.org/`.

[7]`www.appveyor.com/`.

Once the CI server knows which tests to execute, and in which environments, it typically delegates the actual test runs to worker nodes. The worker nodes then report their results back to the server, which takes care of sending notifications and making the outputs and results available for inspection through a web interface.

3.2 Getting Started with Jenkins

First, you need a working Jenkins installation. The official web site[8] contains instructions on how to install and set up Jenkins on all common operating systems. Following, you can also find quick instructions to get a Docker-based Jenkins playground running.

Run Jenkins in Docker

Usually, in a production environment, you'd run the Jenkins server on one machine and have several build workers on different (virtual) machines. For the sake of easy setup, we'll forego this sensible distinction and run the server and all build jobs within the same Docker container, just to have fewer docker containers to manage.

To do this, we use the official Docker image from Jenkins but add the tox Python module (which we will use to create reproducible build environments), as well as the Python version we want to test under.

This customization is done through a custom Dockerfile, which looks like this:

```
FROM jenkins/jenkins:lts
USER root
RUN apt-get update \
    && apt-get install -y python-pip python3.5 \
    && rm -rf /var/lib/apt/lists/*
RUN pip install tox
```

---

[8]https://jenkins.io/download/.

To build the custom image, you must have Docker installed, and your user must have access to the Docker daemon, which on UNIX-based systems works by adding the user to the docker group and logging in anew. The build looks like this:

```
$ docker build -t jenkins-python .
```

This first downloads the image jenkins/jenkins:lts from Dockerhub, which might take a few minutes. Then it runs the commands from the RUN lines of the Dockerfile, which installs pip and then tox. The resulting image gets the name jenkins-python.

Next, start this custom image by running

```
$ docker run --rm -p 8080:8080 -p 50000:50000 \
    -v jenkins_home:/var/jenkins_home jenkins-python
```

The -v ... argument attaches a volume, which makes the Jenkins server not lose state when the container is killed and restarted.

During startup, the container produces output like this on the console:

```
Please use the following password to proceed to installation:

b1792b6c4c324f358a2173bd698c35cd
```

Copy the password, then point your browser to http://127.0.0.1:8080/ and follow the setup instructions (which require the password as the first step). When it comes to plug-ins, add the *Python Plugin* to the list of plug-ins to be installed.

The plug-in installation process can again take a few minutes. After that, you have a working Jenkins server.

Configure a Source Code Repository

Jenkins runs jobs based on source code in a source control repository. For a proper software development project, you likely already have a place where you store the code. If not, you can use one of the many cloud hosting services, such as GitHub,[9] GitLab,[10] or Atlassian's Bitbucket.[11] You can also install GitLab, Gitea,[12] Gogs,[13] or other Git management projects on your own infrastructure.

In either case, you end up with a Git repository that is reachable through the network, which is exactly what Jenkins needs. For the sake of demonstration, I've created a public GitHub repository at `https://github.com/python-ci-cd/python-webcount`.

In the case of private repositories, you also need either an SSH key pair or a combination of username and password, to access the repository.

Creating the First Jenkins Job

We want Jenkins to regularly run the tests of our project. To this end, we need to create a *job*, which configures all of the details on where and how Jenkins gets the source code and runs the tests.

To create a job, click the New Item link in the left column of the Jenkins starting page. Then, you have to enter a name, for example, the name of the repository, `python-webcount`, and a job type, here Multi-configuration project. Then click OK to proceed.

---

[9]`https://github.com/`.
[10]`https://about.gitlab.com/`.
[11]`https://bitbucket.org/`.
[12]`https://gitea.io/en-us/`.
[13]`https://gogs.io/`.

The next screen offers a plethora of configuration options. The following are essential to get our sample job running:

- Select Git in the section Source Code Management, and enter the repository URL (for example, `https://github.com/python-ci-cd/python-webcount.git`). For private repositories, you must also enter valid credentials below the URL (Figure 3-1).

- In the Build Trigger section, select Poll SCM and enter the string `H/5 * * * *` as the schedule, which means polling every five minutes.

- Under Configuration Matrix, add a User-defined Axis with name `TOXENV` and value `py35`. If you have more Python versions installed in Jenkins and defined in the project's `tox.ini` file, you can add them here, separated by spaces (Figure 3-2).

- In the Build section, select Execute Python script and paste the following short Python script into the script area (Figure 3-3).

```python
import os, tox

os.chdir(os.getenv("WORKSPACE"))
tox.cmdline()
```

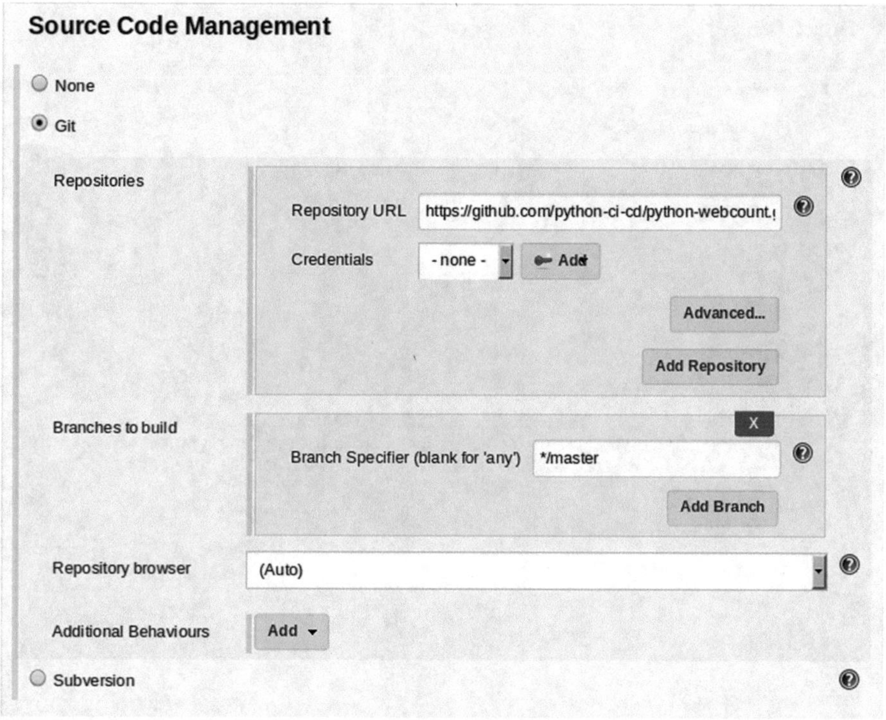

Source Code Management

○ None

⦿ Git

Repositories

Repository URL   https://github.com/python-ci-cd/python-webcount.

Credentials   - none -   🔑 Add

Advanced...

Add Repository

Branches to build

X

Branch Specifier (blank for 'any')   */master

Add Branch

Repository browser   (Auto)

Additional Behaviours   Add ▾

○ Subversion

Figure 3-1. *Jenkins configuration: Source Code Management*

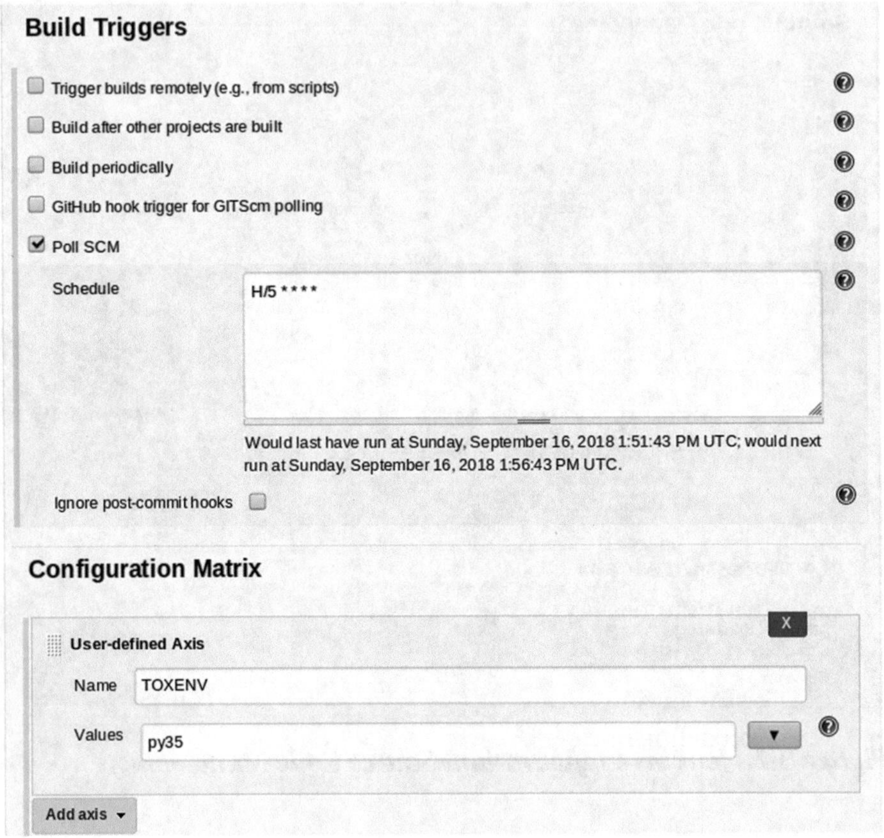

Build Triggers

☐ Trigger builds remotely (e.g., from scripts)   ❔

☐ Build after other projects are built   ❔

☐ Build periodically   ❔

☐ GitHub hook trigger for GITScm polling   ❔

☑ Poll SCM   ❔

Schedule   H/5 * * * *   ❔

Would last have run at Sunday, September 16, 2018 1:51:43 PM UTC; would next
run at Sunday, September 16, 2018 1:56:43 PM UTC.

Ignore post-commit hooks ☐   ❔

Configuration Matrix

X

⠿ **User-defined Axis**

Name   TOXENV

Values   py35   ▼   ❔

Add axis ▼

Figure 3-2. *Jenkins configuration: Build Triggers and Configuration Matrix*

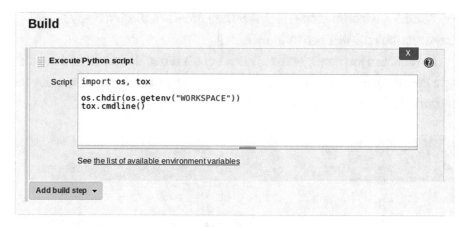

Figure 3-3. *Jenkins configuration: Build configuration*

When you've added these pieces of information, you can save the page and have a first working CI job.

Every five minutes, Jenkins will now check the Git repository for new commits, and if there are any, it will fetch them, run the tests through tox, and make the status available in the front end.

When you define more tox environments, Jenkins shows you whether the test passes or fails per environment and gives you a history for each environment.

3.3 Exporting More Test Details to Jenkins

In its current state, Jenkins detects test status purely based on the exit code of the script that runs, which doesn't provide good granularity. We can improve the granularity by instructing tox to write a machine-readable summary and getting Jenkins to read this data.

To that end, change the commands = pytest line in the tox.ini file in the project's Git repository to

```
commands = pytest --junitxml=junit-{envname}.xml
```

For the environment py35, pytest then creates a file `junit-py35.xml` that describes the test run in more detail.

In Jenkins's job configuration, click Post-build actions and add one of type Publish JUnit test result report. In the field Test report XMLs, enter the pattern `**/junit-*.xml`. (See Figure 3-4.)

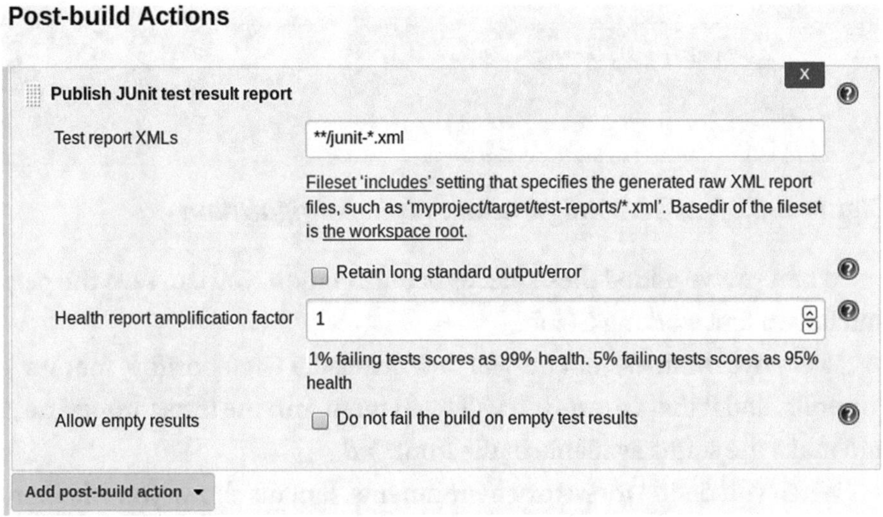

Figure 3-4. *Post-build action: Publish JUnit test result report*

When the job runs again, Jenkins picks up the status of individual test functions and even reports runtimes for each function. This allows a much better diagnostic directly from the Jenkins web interface.

3.4 Patterns for Working with Jenkins

Now that the basics for testing with Jenkins are in place, it's time to think about how you would actually work with it on a day-to-day basis. Most of that is centered on keeping the tests green, that is, all the tests passing. Experience shows that if you don't focus on keeping your jobs green, developers get used to having failing tests and then slip from just 1% failing tests to the test runs becoming pure noise, hence losing their value.

In addition, you should make a review of the tests part of your development workflow, to ensure that tests accurately reflect the requirements, even when a new feature changed the requirements.

Responsibilities

If several developers work on the same code base, it is essential to define clear responsibilities for passing the test suite. Typically, the one who breaks the test suite, as measured by going from green to red in Jenkins, is responsible for fixing it again.

In a team that works like a well-oiled machine, that one rule might be enough. If that's not the case, it can make sense to appoint a *build master* who takes on the primary responsibility for a green test suite.

This doesn't mean that the build master has to clean up all the failing tests. It is more of a managerial role of talking to those who broke the test suite and making sure they clean up after themselves. If that doesn't turn out to be practical, revert the commits that caused trouble and schedule it for re-inclusion when it passes all tests.

The build master role can also rotate between different developers, if nobody feels the calling of always doing it.

Notifications

Notifications can help a development team to keep the tests green, simply by informing the members about broken tests, thus letting them know that an action is required. The notification can be by e-mail, to a chat system that the developers use, or even to a monitor that is physically present in the developer's office. Jenkins's rich ecosystem of plug-ins cover nearly all notification technologies commonly in use.

If you configure Jenkins to send notifications when test suites break, also configure it to send notifications when it passes again. Otherwise, everybody involved will learn to hate notifications from Jenkins giving only negative feedback, which is not a good position for a successful CI process.

Feature Branches and Pull Requests

If your development workflow is based on feature branches and, possibly, merge requests or pull requests (wherein a second person reviews and merges the changes), it makes sense to cover those branches in your CI system as well. The developer who is in charge of merging the branch can then do so in the knowledge that all tests still pass on the feature branch.

In the case of formal merge requests or pull requests, Git hosting solutions such as GitHub and GitLab even support a mode in which the request can only be merged if all tests are passing. In such a scenario, it makes sense to test not just the feature branch but the result of a merge between the feature branch and the development branch. This avoids the situation in which all tests pass both in the development branch and in the feature branch, but the merge breaks some tests.

Such integrations are available for Jenkins as plug-ins.[14]

3.5 Other Metrics in Jenkins

Once a team works smoothly with a CI system, you can use it to gather other metrics about the software and steer it into a desirable direction. Be careful to introduce such metrics only in limited experiments and expand them to larger projects only if you find that they provide tangible value to the development process. They all come with the cost of maintenance and of reducing the developer's autonomy.

---

[14]https://github.com/jenkinsci/gitlab-plugin/wiki/Setup-Example.

Code Coverage

Code coverage measures the percentage of statements or expressions in a piece of source code that is executed during test runs, compared to the total number of expressions. Code coverage serves as a simple proxy for how thorough a test suite exercises the code, though it should be taken with a grain of salt, because combinatoric explosion of path numbers through a piece of code can lead to undetected bugs, even in tested code.

The pytest-cov[15] project gathers such data, and you can even use it to make your CI jobs fail, if the test coverage falls below a certain threshold.

Complexity

There are various attempts at measuring the complexity of a code base, for example, *cyclomatic complexity* and *maintainability index*, which a tool called radon[16] can calculate for Python code. While those numbers aren't too reliable, observing their trend can give you some insight into the health of a code base.

Coding Style

When a project defines a coding style, it can use a tool like pylint[17] or Flake8[18] to check that the code in the repository actually adheres to the guidelines and even fail the build if violations are detected. These two tools come with a set of default rules but can be customized to your own rules.

---

[15]https://pytest-cov.readthedocs.io/en/latest/.

[16]https://radon.readthedocs.io/en/latest/intro.html.

[17]https://pypi.org/project/pylint/.

[18]http://flake8.pycqa.org/en/latest/.

Architectural Constraint Checking

If a project follows a well-defined architecture, there might be rules for the code that can be checked programmatically. For example, a closed three-layer system consisting of user interface (UI), business logic, and storage back end might have rules such as the following:

- UI may not use the storage back end directly, only business logic.

- The storage back end may not use the UI directly.

If those layers are handled as modules in Python code, you can write a small script that analyzes the import statements in all source files and checks if any of them violate these rules. A static import analyzer such as snakefood[19] can make this easier.

Such a tool should make the CI step fail when a violation is detected. This allows you to track whether the ideas of an architecture are actually implemented in the code and prevent the code from slowly weakening the underlying architecture principles.

3.6 Summary

Jenkins is a CI server that automatically runs test suites for you, usually for every new commit in a source repository. This gives you an objective view of the state of your test suite, possibly on multiple Python versions or platforms.

Once you have this view, you can have a process whereby the test suite is always kept passing, and you can derive value from the test suite.

When a mature team works well with a CI process, you can introduce other metrics, such as code coverage or adherence to architectural rules, into the CI process.

---

[19]http://furius.ca/snakefood/.

CHAPTER 4

Continuous Delivery

Continuous integration (CI) is a cornerstone of robust, modern software development, but it is not the pinnacle of the software development methodology. Rather, it is an enabler for more advanced techniques.

When a CI job shows all tests passing, you can be reasonably certain that the software works on its own. But does it work well with other software? How do we get it in front of the end users? This is where continuous delivery (CD) comes in.

When you practice CD, you automate the deployment process of your software and repeat it in several environments. You can use some of these environments for automated tests, such as full-system integration tests, automated acceptance tests, and even performance and penetration tests. Of course, this does not preclude manual Q&A, which can still discover a class of defects that automated tests tend not to catch. Finally, you use the same automation to deploy the software in your production environment, where it reaches its end users.

Setting up a CD system certainly sounds like a daunting task, and it can be. The benefits, however, are numerous, but maybe not all of them are obvious at once.

The rest of this chapter discusses the benefits of CD and provides a rough roadmap to implement it. The rest of the book is dedicated to showing simple approaches to CD and examples that implement it.

© Moritz Lenz 2019
M. Lenz, *Python Continuous Integration and Delivery*,
https://doi.org/10.1007/978-1-4842-4281-0_4

4.1 Reasons for CD and Automated Deployments

Because implementing CD can be a lot of work, it is good to be clear about the reasons and potential benefits of doing so. You can also use the arguments made in this section to convince your management to invest in this approach.

Time Savings

In medium to large organizations, applications and their infrastructure are typically developed and operated by separate teams. Each deployment must be coordinated between these teams. A change request must be filed, a date must be found that suits both teams, information about the new version must be propagated (such as what new configuration is available or required), the development team must make the binaries available for installation, and so on. All of this can easily consume hours or days of time for each release, both in the development team and in the operations team.

Then the actual deployment process also takes its time, often accompanied by downtimes. And since downtimes are often to be avoided during business hours, the deployments must occur during the night or weekend, making the operations team less eager to perform the task. Precious goodwill is also used up by manual deployments.

Automating deployments can save much time and goodwill. For example, Etsy[1] introduced continuous (and, thus, automated) delivery, reducing the deployment time costs from 6–14 hours by a "deployment army" to a 15-minute effort by a single person.[2]

---

[1]www.etsy.com/.

[2]Mike Britain, "Principles and Practices in Continuous Deployment at Etsy," SlideShare, www.slideshare.net/mikebrittain/principles-and-practices-in-continuous-deployment-at-etsy, April 2, 2014.

Shorter Release Cycles

It is a truism that tasks that take a lot of effort are done much less frequently than those that require virtually no effort. The same is true of risky endeavors: we tend to avoid doing them often.

Companies that do manual releases and deployments often do releases weekly or even less frequently. Some do monthly or even quarterly releases. In more conservative industries, even doing releases every 6 or 12 months is not unheard of.

Infrequent releases invariably lead to drawn-out development processes and slow time-to-market. If software is deployed once every quarter, the time from specification to deployment can easily be dominated by the slow release cycle, at least for small features.

This can mean, for example, that an online business with a bad user experience in the checkout process must wait about three months to improve the user experience, which can cost real money. Automating the deployment makes it easier to release more frequently, alleviating this pain.

Shorter Feedback Cycles

The best way to get feedback for software is to deploy it to the production environment. There, people will actually use it, and you can then listen to what they have to say or even continuously measure their engagement with different parts of the system.

If you are developing tools for internal use in a company, you might get a few people to try them out in a staging environment, but that's not easy. It takes time from their actual work; the staging environment must be set up with all the necessary data (customer data, inventory, ...) even to be usable; and then all the changes there will be lost eventually. In my experience, getting users to test in a non-production environment is hard work and only worth it for major changes.

With manual and, thus, infrequent releases, the feedback cycle is slow, which goes against the whole idea of an "agile" or "lean" development process.

ℹ Lean software development is a development paradigm inspired by Toyota's lean manufacturing process, which focuses on reducing unnecessary work, delivering software fast, learning, and related principles.

Because human communication is prone to misunderstandings, the first implementation of a feature seldom fulfills the original expectations. Feedback cycles are inevitable. Slow release cycles thus lead to slow development, frustrating both the stakeholders and the developers.

But there are secondary effects too. When improvement cycles take a long time, many users won't even bother to request small improvements at all. This is a real pity, because a good user interface is made of hundreds of small conveniences and sharp edges that must be rounded. So, in the long run, slow release cycles lead to worse usability and quality.

Reliability of Releases

There is a vicious cycle with manual releases. They tend to be infrequent, which means that many changes go into a single release. This increases the risk of something going wrong. When a big release causes too much trouble, managers and engineers look for ways to improve the reliability of the next release, by adding more verification steps, more process.

But more process means more effort, and more effort leads to even slower cycles, leading to even more changes per release. You can see where this is going.

Automating steps of the release process, or even the whole process, is a way to break this vicious cycle. Computers are much better than humans at following instructions to the letter, and their concentration doesn't slip at the end of a long night of deploying software.

Once the release process has become more reliable and quicker to execute, it's easy to push for more frequent releases, each of which introduces fewer changes. The time saved by automation frees resources to further improve the automated release process.

With doing more deployments also comes more experience, which puts you into a good position to improve the process and tools even further.

Smaller Increments Make Triaging Easier

When a deployment introduces a bug, and that deployment introduced only one or two features or bug fixes, it is usually pretty easy to figure out which change caused the bug (triaging). In contrast, when many changes are part of the same deployment, it is much harder to triage new bugs, which means more time wasted, but this also leads to a longer time until defects can be repaired.

More Architectural Freedom

Current trends in the software industry are moving away from huge, monolithic applications toward distributed systems of more and smaller components. This is what the *microservice* pattern is all about. Smaller applications or services tend to be easier to maintain, and scalability requirements demand that they must each be able to run on different machines, and often on several machines per service.

But if deploying one application or service is already a pain, deploying ten or even a hundred smaller applications promises to be a much bigger pain and makes it downright irresponsible to mix microservices with manual deployment.

Automatic deployments thus open up the space of possible software architectures that you can utilize to solve a business problem.

Advanced Quality Assurance Techniques

Once you have the necessary infrastructure, you can employ amazing strategies for QA. For example, GitHub uses live, parallel execution of new and old implementations[3] to avoid regressions, both on the result and performance parameters.

Imagine you develop a travel search engine, and you want to improve the search algorithm. You could deploy both the old and new version of the engine at the same time and run the incoming queries (or a fraction of them) against both and define some metrics by which to evaluate them. For example, fast travel and low costs make a good flight connection. You can use this to find cases in which the new engine performs worse than the old one and use this data to improve it. You can also use this data to demonstrate the superiority of the new search engine, thus justifying the efforts spent developing it.

But such experiments are not practical if each new version must be deployed manually and deploying each version is a major effort. Automatic deployment does not give you these benefits automatically, but it is a prerequisite for employing such advanced QA techniques.

---

[3]Vicent Martí, "Move Fast and Fix Things," GitHub Engineering, http://githubengineering.com/move-fast/, December 15, 2015.

4.2 A Plan for CD

I hope that by now you are convinced that CD is a good idea. When I arrived at that stage, the prospect of actually implementing it seemed quite daunting.

The process of CD can be broken down into a few steps, each of them manageable on its own. Even better, the automation of each step provides benefits, even if the whole process isn't automated yet.

Let's take a look at a typical CD system and the steps involved.

The Pipeline Architecture

A CD system is structured as a pipeline. A new commit or branch in a version control system triggers the instantiation of the pipeline and starts executing the first of a series of stages. When a stage runs successfully, it triggers the next stage. If it fails, the entire pipeline instance stops.

Then manual intervention is necessary, typically by adding a new commit that fixes code or tests or by fixing the environment or the pipeline configuration. A new instance of the pipeline, or a rerun of the failed stage, can then have a chance to succeed.

Deviations from the strict pipeline model are possible. Branches, potentially executed in parallel, for example, allow running different tests in different environments and waiting with the next step until both are completed successfully. Branching into multiple pipelines, and thus parallel execution, is called *fan out*; joining the pipelines into a single branch is called *fan in* (Figure 4-1).

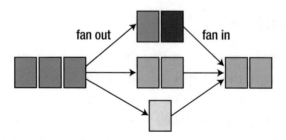

Figure 4-1. *Fan out branches pipelines; fan in joins them*

The typical stages are building, running the unit tests, deployment to a first test environment, running integration tests there, potentially deployment to and tests in various test environments, and, finally, deployment to production (Figure 4-2).

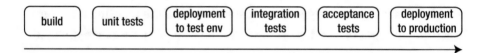

Figure 4-2. *Typical recommended stages for a deployment pipeline*

Sometimes, these stages blur a bit. For example, a typical build of Debian packages also runs the unit tests, which alleviates the need for a separate unit-testing stage. Likewise, if the deployment to an environment runs smoke tests for each host it deploys to, there is no need for a separate smoke test stage (Figure 4-3).

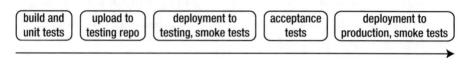

Figure 4-3. *In an actual pipeline, it can be convenient to combine multiple recommended stages into one and possibly have extra stages that the theory glosses over*

Typically, there is a piece of software that controls the flow of the whole pipeline. It prepares the necessary files for a stage, runs the code associated with the stage, collects its output and *artifacts* (that is, files that the stage produces and that are worth keeping, such as binaries or test output), determines whether the stage was successful, and then proceeds to the next stage.

From an architectural standpoint, this relieves the stages from having to know what stage comes next and even how to reach the machine on which it runs. It decouples the stages and maintains separation of concerns.

Anti-Pattern: Separate Builds per Environment

If you use a branch model such as GitFlow[4] for your source code, it is tempting to automatically deploy the develop branch to the testing environment. When the time comes for a release, you merge the development branch into the master branch (possibly through the indirection of separate release branches), and then you automatically build the master branch and deploy the result to the production environment.

It is tempting, because it is a straightforward extension of an existing, proven workflow. *Don't do it.*

The big problem with this approach is that you don't actually test what's going to be deployed, and on the flip side, you deploy something untested to production. Even if you have a staging environment before deploying to production, you are invalidating all the testing you did, if you don't actually ship the binary or package that you tested in previous environments.

---

[4]Vincent Driessen, "A Successful Git Branching Model," nvie.com, http://nvie.com/posts/a-successful-git-branching-model/, January 5, 2010.

If you build "testing" and "release" packages from different sources (such as different branches), the resulting binaries will differ. Even if you use the exact same source, building twice is still a bad idea, because many builds aren't reproducible. Nondeterministic compiler behavior and differences in environments and dependencies all can lead to packages that worked fine in one build and failed in another. It is best to avoid such potential differences and errors by deploying to production exactly the same build that you tested in the testing environments.

Differences in behavior between the environments, where they are desirable, should be implemented by configuration that is not part of the build. It should also be self-evident that the configuration must be under version control and deployed automatically. There are tools that specialize in deploying configuration, such as Puppet, Chef, and Ansible, and later chapters discuss how to integrate them into the deployment process.

Everything Hinges on the Packaging Format

Building a deployable artifact is an early stage in a CD pipeline: build, repository management, installation, and operation all depend on the choice of package format. Python software is usually packaged as a source tarball, in a format determined by the `setuptools` package, and sometimes as a binary *wheel* package, specified by the Python Enhancement Proposal (PEP) 427.[5]

Neither source tarballs nor wheels are particularly suitable for deploying a running application. They lack hooks during installation time for creating necessary system resources (such as user accounts), for starting or restarting applications, and other operating system–specific tasks. They also don't have support for managing non-Python dependencies, such as a database's client libraries written in C.

---

[5]Python Software Foundation, "PEP 427—The Wheel Binary Package Format 1.0," `www.python.org/dev/peps/pep-0427/`, 2018.

Python packages are installed by the *pip* package manager, which defaults to a system-wide, global installation, which sometimes interacts poorly with Python packages installed by the operating system's package manager. Workarounds exist, for example, in the form of virtual environment, but managing these requires extra care and effort.

Finally, in the case of separate development and operating responsibilities, the operating team usually is much more familiar with native operating system packages. Nonetheless, source tarballs serve a very useful role as the starting point for creating packages in formats that are more suitable for direct deployment.

In this book, we deploy to Debian GNU/Linux machines, and so we build Debian packages, using a two-step process. First, we create a source tarball using a `setup.py` file powered by `setuptools`. Then the tool `dh-virtualenv` creates a Debian package that contains a virtualenv, into which the software and all of its Python dependencies are installed.

Technology for Managing Debian Repositories

Deploying Debian (and most other) packages works by uploading them into a *repository*. Target machines are then configured with the URL of this repository. From the perspective of the target machines, this is a pull-based model, which allows them to fetch dependencies that aren't installed yet. These repositories consist of a certain directory layout, in which files of predefined names and formats contain metadata and link to the actual package files.

These files and directories can be exposed by transport mechanisms, such as local file access (and possibly mounted through a networked file system), HTTP, and FTP. HTTP is good choice, because it is simple to set up, easy to debug, and isn't usually a performance bottleneck, because it's a standard system component.

Various software exists to manage Debian repositories, much of which is poorly documented or barely maintained. Some solutions, such as *debarchiver,* or *dak,* offer remote upload through SSH but don't give immediate feedback as to whether the upload was successful. Debarchiver also processes uploaded files in batches, triggered by a cron job, which leads to a delay that makes automation much less fun.

I settled on *Aptly,*[6] which is a command-line toolset for managing repositories. When you add a new package to the repository, Aptly gives immediate feedback in the form of an exit code. It does not provide a convenient way to upload the files onto the server in which the repositories lie, but that is something that the pipeline manager can do.

Finally, Aptly can keep multiple versions of the same package in a repository, which makes it much easier to do a rollback to a previous version.

Tooling for Installing Packages

Once you have built a Debian package, uploaded it into a repository, and have the target machine configured to use this repository, interactive package installation looks like this:

```
$ apt-get update && apt-get install $package
```

There are some subtleties to be aware of in automated installations. You must switch off all forms of interactivity, possibly control the verbosity of the output, configure whether downgrades are acceptable, and so on.

---

[6]www.aptly.info/.

Instead of trying to figure out all these details, it is a good idea to reuse an existing tool whose authors have already done the hard work. Configuration-management tools such as Ansible,[7] Chef,[8] Puppet,[9] Salt,[10] and Rex[11] have modules for installing packages, so they can be a good choice.

Not all configuration management systems are suitable for automating deployments, however. Puppet is usually used in a pull-based model, in which each Puppet-managed machine periodically contacts a server and asks for its target configuration. That is great for scalability but makes integration into a workflow a major pain. Push-based models, in which the manager contacts the managed machine—for example, through SSH— and then executes a command, are much better suited for deployment tasks (and typically offer a simpler and more pleasant development and debugging experience).

For this book, I've chosen Ansible. This is mostly because I like its declarative syntax, its simple model, and that a bit of googling has found good solutions to all practical problems so far.

Controlling the Pipeline

Even if you think of a deployment pipeline in terms of building, testing, distributing, and installing software, much of the work done is actually "glue," that is, small tasks that make the whole thing run smoothly. These include polling the version control system, preparing the directories for the

---

[7]https://ansible.com.
[8]www.chef.io/.
[9]https://puppet.com/.
[10]www.saltstack.com/.
[11]www.rexify.org/.

build jobs, collecting the built packages (or aborting the current pipeline instance on failure), and distributing the work to the machines that are most appropriate for the task.

Of course, there are tools for these tasks as well. General CI and build servers such as Jenkins typically can do the job. But there are also tools specialized in CD pipelines, such as Go continuous delivery (GoCD)[12] and Concourse.[13]

While Jenkins is a great CI tool, its job-centric worldview makes it less optimal for the pipeline model of CD. Here, we will explore GoCD, which is open source software by ThoughtWorks, Inc. It is written primarily in Java and is available for most operating systems. Conveniently for the Debian-based development environment, it offers pre-built Debian packages.

In the examples in the upcoming chapters, we'll package a build that also runs the unit tests. In a production setting, you'd likely include a post-build action in the Jenkins pipeline that uses the GoCD API to trigger the CD steps, if all the tests in Jenkins have passed.

4.3 Summary

CD enables deployment of software in small increments. This reduces time to market, shortens feedback cycles, and makes it easier to triage newly introduced bugs.

The steps involved in CD include unit testing, package building, package distribution, installation, and testing of the installed packages. It is controlled by a pipeline system, for which we will use GoCD.

---

[12]www.gocd.org/.

[13]https://concourse-ci.org/.

CHAPTER 5

Building Packages

We will first explore the basics of creating Python source tarballs and then the creation of Debian packages from those tarballs.

5.1 Creating a Python Source Tarball

To create a Python source tarball, you have to write a `setup.py` script that uses `distutils` or `setuptools`. Then `python setup.py sdist` creates the tarball in the right format.

   `distutils` is part of the Python standard library but lacks some commonly used features. `setuptools` adds these features by extending `distutils`. Which of these tools you use is mostly a matter of taste and context.

   Here is a pretty minimal `setup.py` file using `setuptools` for the webcount example from Chapter 2.

```
from setuptools import setup

setup(
    name = "webcount",
    version = "0.1",
    packages=['webcount', 'test'],
    install_requires=['requests'],
)
```

© Moritz Lenz 2019
M. Lenz, *Python Continuous Integration and Delivery*,
https://doi.org/10.1007/978-1-4842-4281-0_5

This imports the setup function from setuptools and calls it with metadata about the package—name, version, the list of Python packages to include, and a list of dependencies.

The setuptools documentation[1] lists other arguments you can pass to the setup function. The ones used most often include

- Author: Used for the maintainer's names. author_ email is for a contact's e-mail address.

- url: This should be a link to the project's web site.

- package_data: Used for adding non-Python files to the tarball.

- description: This is for a one-paragraph description of the package's purpose.

- python_requires: Used to specify what Python versions your package supports.

- scripts: This can hold a list of Python files that are installed as runnable scripts, not just Python packages.

When the setup.py file is in place, you can run python setup.py sdist, and it creates a tarball in the dist directory. The file is named like the name in setup.py, followed by a dash, the version number, and then the suffix .tar.gz. In our example, it's dist/webcount-0.1.tar.gz.

5.2 Debian Packaging with dh-virtualenv

The official Debian repositories come with more than 40,000 software packages and include software written in all common programming languages. To support this scale and diversity, tooling has been developed

---

[1]https://setuptools.readthedocs.io/en/latest/setuptools.html#basic-use.

to make it easy to get started with packaging but also supports many hooks for customization.

This tooling, which mostly lives in the devscripts package, reads files from the debian directory for metadata and build instructions.

While a complete description of the debhelper tooling would be a big enough topic for a separate book, I want to provide enough information here to get you started.

Getting Started with Packaging

The dh-make package provides a tool for creating a skeleton debian directory, with some metadata already filled in and sample files to base your own versions on. The rest of the tooling then utilizes the files inside the debian packages, to build a binary archive from your source code.

If you are following this example in your own development environment, ensure that the dh-make package is installed before continuing.

The starting point for a Debian developer is typically a tar archive with source code that another project released, which the Debian community calls *upstream*. With the sample project from the previous chapter, we are our own upstream and use a Git repository instead of a tarball, so we must instruct dh_make to build its own "original" tarball, as follows:

```
$ dh_make --packageclass=s –yes --createorig \
    -p python-webcount_0.1
Maintainer Name    : Moritz Lenz
Email-Address      : moritz@unknown
Date               : Tue, 04 Sep 2018 15:04:35 +0200
Package Name       : python-webcount
Version            : 0.1
License            : blank
Package Type       : single
```

Currently there is not top level Makefile. This may require additional tuning Done. Please edit the files in the debian/ subdirectory now.

5.3 The control File

debian/control has metadata about the source package and potentially multiple binary packages built from this source package. For the python-webcount project, after a few small edits, it looks like Listing 5-1.

Listing 5-1. File debian/control: Metadata for the Debian Package

```
Source: python-webcount

Section: unknown
Priority: optional
Maintainer: Moritz Lenz <moritz@unknown>
Build-Depends: debhelper (>= 10), dh-virtualenv
Standards-Version: 4.1.2

Package: python-webcount
Architecture: any
Depends: python3
Description: Count occurrences of words in a web page
```

This declares the build dependency dh-virtualenv, which you need to install, in order to build the Debian package.

Directing the Build Process

The Debian maintainers use the command dpkg-buildpackage or debuild to build the Debian package. Among other things, these tools invoke the debian/rules script with the current action as the argument. The action can be such things as configure, build, test, or install.

Typically, debian/rules is a makefile, with a catchall target % that invokes dh, the debhelper. The minimal debian/rules script looks like this:

```
#!/usr/bin/make -f
%:
        dh $@
```

We must extend this to invoke dh-virtualenv and to tell dh-virtualenv to use Python 3 as the basis for its installation.

```
%:
        dh $@ --with python-virtualenv

override_dh_virtualenv:
        dh_virtualenv --python=/usr/bin/python3
```

Being a makefile, the indentation here must be actual tabulator characters, not a series of spaces.

Declaring Python Dependencies

dh-virtualenv expects a file called requirements.txt, which lists the Python dependencies, each one on a separate line (Listing 5-2).

Listing 5-2. File requirements.txt

```
flask
pytest
gunicorn
```

These lines will be passed to pip on the command line, so specifying version numbers works just as in pip, for example, pytest==3.8.0. You can use a line like

```
--index-url=https://...
```

to specify a URL to your own pypi mirror, which dh-virtualenv then uses to fetch the packages.

Building the Package

Once these files are in place, you can trigger the build using this command:

```
$ dpkg-buildpackage -b -us -uc
```

The -b option instructs dpkg-buildpackage to only build the binary package (which is the deployable unit we want), and -us and -uc skip the signing process that Debian developers use to upload their packages to the Debian mirrors.

The command must be invoked in the root directory of the project (so, the directory that contains the debian directory), and when successful, it puts the generated .deb file into the parent directory of the root directory.

Creating the python-matheval Package

Packaging matheval as the Debian package python-matheval works similarly to webcount. The main difference is that matheval is a service that should be running all the time.

We use systemd,[2] the init system used by Debian, Ubuntu, and many other Linux distributions, to control the service process. This is done by writing a *unit file*, stored as debian/python-matheval.service.

```
[Unit]
Description=Evaluates mathematical expressions
Requires=network.target
After=network.target

[Service]
```

---

[2]Wikipedia, "systemd," https://en.wikipedia.org/wiki/Systemd, 2018.

```
Type=simple
SyslogIdentifier=python-matheval
User=nobody
ExecStart=/usr/share/python-custom/python-matheval/bin/\
gunicorn --bind 0.0.0.0:8800 matheval.frontend:app

PrivateTmp=yes
InaccessibleDirectories=/home
ReadOnlyDirectories=/bin /sbin /usr /lib /etc

[Install]
WantedBy=multi-user.target
```

Managing systemd unit files is a standard task for Debian packages, and so a helper tool exists that does it for us: dh-systemd. We must have it installed and declare it as a build dependency in the control file (Listing 5-3).

Listing 5-3. debian/control File for the python-matheval Package

```
Source: python-matheval
Section: main
Priority: optional
Maintainer: Moritz Lenz <moritz.lenz@gmail.com>
Build-Depends: debhelper (>=9), dh-virtualenv,
              dh-systemd, python-setuptools
Standards-Version: 3.9.6

Package: python-matheval
Architecture: any
Depends: python3 (>= 3.4)
Description: Web service that evaluates math expressions.
```

The debian/rules file similarly requires a --with systemd argument.

```
#!/usr/bin/make -f
export DH_VIRTUALENV_INSTALL_ROOT=/usr/share/python-custom

%:
        dh $@ --with python-virtualenv --with systemd

override_dh_virtualenv:
        dh_virtualenv --python=/usr/bin/python3 --setuptools-test
```

Together, the familiar dpkg-buildpackage invocation creates a Debian package that, on installation, automatically starts the web service and restarts it when a new version of the package is installed.

Tradeoffs of dh-virtualenv

The dh-virtualenv tool makes it pretty easy to create Debian packages with all Python dependencies packaged into them. This is very convenient for the developer, because it means he/she can start using Python packages without having to create separate Debian packages from them.

It also means that you can depend on several different versions of Python packages in multiple applications installed on the same machine—something you cannot easily do if you use the system-wide Python packages.

On the other hand, this "fat packaging" means that if one of the Python packages contains a security flaw, or an otherwise critical bug, you must rebuild and deploy all Debian packages that contain a copy of the flawed code.

Finally, dh-virtualenv packages are tied to the Python version that was used on the build server. So, if a package is built for Python 3.5, for example, it won't work with Python 3.6. If you are transitioning from one Python version to the next, you have to build packages for both in parallel.

5.4 Summary

We build packages in two steps: first, a Python source tarball based on Python `setuptools`, then a binary Debian package through `dh-virtualenv`. Both steps use a few files, mostly based on declarative syntax. The end result is a mostly self-contained Debian package that just needs a matching Python version installed on the target machine.

CHAPTER 6

Distributing Debian Packages

Once a Debian package is built, it must be distributed to the servers it is to be installed on. Debian, as well as basically all other operating systems, uses a pull model for that. The package and its metadata are stored on a server that the client can communicate with and request the metadata and the package.

The sum of metadata and packages is called a *repository*. In order to distribute packages to the servers that need them, we must set up and maintain such a repository.

6.1 Signatures

In Debian land, packages are cryptographically signed, to ensure they aren't tampered with on the repository server or during transmission. Thus, the first step is to create a key pair that is used to sign this particular repository. (If you already have a PGP key for signing packages, you can skip this step.)

The following assumes that you are working with a pristine system user that does not have a GnuPG key ring yet and will be used to maintain the Debian repository. It also assumes that you have the gnupg package installed in version 2 or later versions.

© Moritz Lenz 2019
M. Lenz, *Python Continuous Integration and Delivery*,
https://doi.org/10.1007/978-1-4842-4281-0_6

First, create a file called `key-control-file-gpg2`, with the following contents:

```
%no-protection
Key-Type: RSA
Key-Length: 1024
Subkey-Type: RSA
Name-Real: Aptly Signing Key
Name-Email: nobody@example.com
Expire-Date: 0
%commit
%echo done
```

Substitute nobody@example.com with your own e-mail address or an e-mail address for the project you are working for, then run the following command:

```
$ gpg --gen-key --batch key-control-file-gpg2
```

The output of this command contains a line like the following:

```
gpg: key D163C61A6C25A6B7 marked as ultimately trusted
```

The string of hex digits D163C... is the key ID, and this differs for every run. Use it to export the public key, which we'll need later on.

```
$ gpg --export --armor D163C61A6C25A6B7 > pubkey.asc
```

6.2 Preparing the Repository

I use Aptly[1] for creating and managing the repository. It is a command-line application with no server component.

---

[1]`www.aptly.info/`.

To initialize a repository, I first have to come up with a name. Here, I call it myrepo.

```
$ aptly repo create -distribution=stretch \
    -architectures=amd64,i386,all -component=main myrepo

Local repo [myrepo] successfully added.
You can run 'aptly repo add myrepo ...' to add packages
to repository.

$ aptly publish repo -architectures=amd64,i386,all myrepo
Warning: publishing from empty source, architectures list
should be complete, it can't be changed after publishing
(use -architectures flag)
Loading packages...
Generating metadata files and linking package files...
Finalizing metadata files...
Signing file 'Release' with gpg, please enter your
passphrase when prompted:
Clearsigning file 'Release' with gpg, please enter your
passphrase when prompted:

Local repo myrepo has been successfully published.
Please set up your webserver to serve directory
'/home/aptly/.aptly/public' with autoindexing.
Now you can add following line to apt sources:
  deb http://your-server/ stretch main
Don't forget to add your GPG key to apt with apt-key.

You can also use `aptly serve` to publish your repositories
over HTTP quickly.
```

Now that the repository has been created, you can add a package by running

```
$ aptly repo add myrepo python_webcount_0.1-1_all.deb
$ aptly publish update myrepo
```

This updates the files in .aptly/public to be a valid Debian repository that includes the newly added package.

6.3 Automating Repository Creation and Package Addition

For use inside the deployment pipeline, it is handy to have the repositories, and the addition of packages to these repositories, created with a single command. It also makes sense to have separate repositories for the different environments. Hence, we need a repository each for the testing, staging, and production environments. A second dimension is the distribution for which a package is built.

Here is a small program (Listing 6-1) that, given an environment, a distribution, and a list of file names of Debian packages, creates the repository in the path $HOME/aptly/$environment/$distribution, adds the packages, and then updates the public files of the repositories:

Listing 6-1. add-package, a Tool for Creating and Populating Debian Repositories

```
#!/usr/bin/env python3
import json
import os
import os.path
import subprocess
import sys
```

```python
assert len(sys.argv) >= 4, \
    'Usage: add-package <env> <distribution> <.deb-file>+'

env, distribution = sys.argv[1:3]
packages = sys.argv[3:]

base_path = os.path.expanduser('~') + '/aptly'
repo_path = '/'.join((base_path, env, distribution))
config_file = '{}/{}-{}.conf'.format(base_path, env,
                                     distribution)

def run_aptly(*args):
    aptly_cmd = ['aptly', '-config=' + config_file]
    subprocess.call(aptly_cmd + list(args))

def init_config():
    os.makedirs(base_path, exist_ok=True)
    contents = {
        'rootDir': repo_path,
        'architectures': ['amd64', 'all'],
    }
    with open(config_file, 'w') as conf:
        json.dump(contents, conf)

def init_repo():
    if os.path.exists(repo_path + '/db'):
        return
    os.makedirs(repo_path, exist_ok=True)
    run_aptly('repo', 'create',
        '-distribution=' + distribution, 'myrepo')
    run_aptly('publish', 'repo', 'myrepo')
```

```python
def add_packages():
    for pkg in packages:
        run_aptly('repo', 'add', 'myrepo', pkg)
    run_aptly('publish', 'update', distribution)

if __name__ == '__main__':
    init_config();
    init_repo();
    add_packages();
```

It can be used as

```
$ ./add-package testing stretch python-matheval_0.1-1_all.deb
```

to add the python-matheval_0.1-1_all.deb file to the Stretch repository for environment testing, and it automatically creates that repository, if it does not yet exist.

6.4 Serving the Repositories

As is, the repositories are only available on one machine. The easiest way to make them available to more machines is to serve the public directory as static files through HTTP.

If you use Apache as the web server, the virtual host configuration to serve these files could look like Listing 6-2.

Listing 6-2. Apache 2 Configuration for Serving Debian Repositories

```
ServerName apt.example.com
ServerAdmin moritz@example.com

DocumentRoot /home/aptly/aptly/
Alias /debian/testing/stretch/        \
```

```
    /home/aptly/aptly/testing/stretch/public/
Alias /debian/production/stretch/  \
    /home/aptly/aptly/production/stretch/public/
# more repositories go here

Options +Indexes +FollowSymLinks
Require all granted

LogLevel notice
CustomLog /var/log/apache2/apt/access.log combined
ErrorLog /var/log/apache2/apt/error.log
ServerSignature On
```

After creating the logging directory (`mkdir -p /var/log/apache2/apt/`), enabling the virtual host (`a2ensite apt.conf`), and restarting Apache, the Debian repository is ready.

If, instead, you prefer lighttpd,[2] you could use a configuration snippet such as that in Listing 6-3.

Listing 6-3. lighttpd Configuration for Serving Debian Repositories

```
dir-listing.encoding = "utf-8"
server.dir-listing = "enable"
alias.url = (
    "/debian/testing/stretch/"    =>
        "/home/aptly/aptly/testing/stretch/public/",
    "/debian/production/stretch/" =>
        "/home/aptly/aptly/production/stretch/public/",
    # more repositories go here
)
```

---

[2]www.lighttpd.net/.

Configuring a Machine to Use the Repository

When a machine uses one of the new repositories, it first has to trust the cryptographic key with which the repositories are signed.

Copy the PGP public key (pubkey.asc) to the machine that will use the repository and import it.

```
$ apt-key add pubkey.asc
```

Then add the actual package source.

```
$ echo "deb http://apt.example.com/ stretch main" \
  > /etc/apt/source.list.d/myrepo.list
```

After an apt-get update, the contents of the repository are available, and an apt-cache policy python-matheval shows the repository as a possible source for this package.

```
$ apt-cache policy python-webcount
python-webcount:
  Installed: (none)
  Candidate: 0.1-1
  Version table:
*** 0.1-1 0
        990 http://apt.example.com/ stretch/main amd64 Packages
        100 /var/lib/dpkg/status
```

This concludes the whirlwind tour through Debian repository management and, thus, package distribution.

6.5 Summary

Debian package installers such as `apt-get` and `aptitude` from the APT software suite read metadata and download packages from repositories. Software such as Aptly manages these repositories.

Cryptographic signatures authenticate packages and catch man-in-the-middle attacks and transport errors that modify software packages. You must to create a GPG key and supply it to Aptly and configure the target machines to trust this key.

CHAPTER 7

Package Deployment

In the previous chapters, you have seen how Debian packages are built, inserted into a repository, and how this repository can be configured as a package source on a target machine. With these preparations in mind, interactively installing the actual package becomes easy.

To install the python-matheval sample project, run

```
$ apt-get update
$ apt-get install python-matheval
```

on the target machine.

If several machines are required to provide a service, it can be beneficial to coordinate the update, for example, only updating one or two hosts at a time or doing a small integration test on each after moving on to the next. A nice tool for doing that is Ansible,[1] an open source IT automation and configuration management system.

7.1 Ansible: A Primer

Ansible is a very pragmatic and powerful configuration management system that is easy to get started with. If you already know your way around Ansible (or choose to use a different configuration management and deployment system), you can safely skip this section.

---

[1] www.ansible.com/.

© Moritz Lenz 2019
M. Lenz, *Python Continuous Integration and Delivery*,
https://doi.org/10.1007/978-1-4842-4281-0_7

Connections and Inventory

Ansible is typically used to connect to one or more remote machines via Secure Shell (SSH) and bring them into a desired state. The connection method is pluggable. Other methods include local, which simply invokes the commands on the local machine instead, and docker, which connects through the Docker daemon to configure a running container. Ansible calls these remote machines *hosts*.

To tell Ansible where and how to connect, you write an *inventory* or *hosts* file. In the inventory file, you can define hosts and groups of hosts, and also set variables that control how to connect to them (Listing 7-1).

Listing 7-1. File myinventory: an Ansible Hosts File

```
# example inventory file
[all:vars]
# variables set here apply to all hosts
ansible_ssh_user=root

[web]
# a group of webservers
www01.example.com
www02.example.com

[app]
# a group of 5 application servers,
# all following the same naming scheme:
app[01:05].example.com

[frontend:children]
# a group that combines the two previous groups
app
web
```

```
[database]
# here we override ansible_ssh_user for just one host
db01.example.com ansible_ssh_user=postgres
```

See the introduction to inventory files[2] for more information.

To test the connection, you can use the ping module on the command line.

```
$ ansible -i myinventory web -m ping
www01.example.com | success >> {
    "changed": false,
    "ping": "pong"
}

www02.example.com | success >> {
    "changed": false,
    "ping": "pong"
}
```

Let's break the command line down into its components. -i myinventory tells Ansible to use the myinventory file as inventory. web tells Ansible which hosts to work on. It can be a group, as in this example, a single host, or several such things, separated by a colon. For example, www01.example.com:database would select one of the web servers and all the database servers.

Finally, -m ping tells Ansible which module to execute. ping is probably the simplest module. It just sends the response "pong" without conducting any changes on the remote machine, and it is mostly used for debugging the inventory file and credentials.

---

[2]http://docs.ansible.com/ansible/intro_inventory.html.

These commands run in parallel on the different hosts, so the order in which the responses are printed can vary. If a problem occurs when connecting to a host, add the option -vvvv to the command line, to get more output, including any error messages from SSH.

Ansible implicitly gives you the group all, which—you guessed it—contains all the hosts configured in the inventory file.

Modules

Whenever you want to do something on a host through Ansible, you invoke a module to do it. Modules usually take arguments that specify exactly what should happen. On the command line, you can add those arguments with ansible -m module -a 'arguments'. For example:

```
$ ansible -i myinventory database -m shell -a 'echo "hi there"'
db01.example.com | success | rc=0 >>
hi there
```

Ansible comes with a wealth of built-in modules and an ecosystem of third-party modules as well. Most modules are *idempotent*, which means that repeated execution with the same arguments conducts no changes after the first run. For example, instead of instructing Ansible to create a directory, you instruct it to ensure the directory exists. Running such an instruction the first time creates the directory, and running it the second time does nothing, while still reporting success.

Here, I want to present just a few commonly used modules.

The **shell** Module

The shell module[3] executes a shell command on the host and accepts some options, such as chdir, to change into another working directory, before running the command.

---

[3]http://docs.ansible.com/ansible/shell_module.html.

```
$ ansible -i myinventory database -m shell -e 'pwd chdir=/tmp'
db01.example.com | success | rc=0 >>
/tmp
```

This is fairly generic, but it is also an option of last resort. If there is a more specific module for the task at hand, you should prefer the more specific module. For example, you could ensure that system users exist using the shell module, but the more specialized user module[4] is much easier to use for that and likely does a better job than an improvised shell script.

The copy Module

With copy,[5] you can copy files verbatim from the local to the remote machine.

```
$ ansible -i myinventory database -m copy \
      -a 'src=README.md dest=/etc/motd mode=644 db01.example.com'
      | success >> {
    "changed": true,
    "dest": "/etc/motd",
    "gid": 0,
    "group": "root",
    "md5sum": "d41d8cd98f00b204e9800998ecf8427e",
    "mode": "0644",
    "owner": "root",
    "size": 0,
    "state": "file",
    "uid": 0
}
```

---

[4]http://docs.ansible.com/ansible/user_module.html.
[5]http://docs.ansible.com/ansible/copy_module.html.

The `template` Module

template[6] mostly works like copy, but it interprets the source file as a Jinja2 template,[7] before transferring it to the remote host. This is commonly used to create configuration files and incorporate information from variables (more on that later).

Templates cannot be used directly from the command line but, rather, in playbooks, so here is an example of a simple playbook.

```
# file motd.j2
This machine is managed by {{team}}.

# file template-example.yml
---
- hosts: all
  vars:
    team: Slackers
  tasks:
  - template: src=motd.j2 dest=/etc/motd mode=0644
```

More on playbooks later, but what you can see is that this defines a variable team, sets it to the value Slackers, and the template interpolates this variable.

Running the playbook with

```
$ ansible-playbook -i myinventory \
    --limit database template-example.yml
```

creates a file /etc/motd on the database server with the contents

```
This machine is managed by Slackers.
```

---

[6]http://docs.ansible.com/ansible/template_module.html.
[7]http://jinja.pocoo.org/docs/dev/.

The `file` Module

The file module[8] manages attributes of file names, such as permissions, but also allows you to create directories and soft and hard links.

```
$ ansible -i myinventory database -m file \
    -a 'path=/etc/apt/sources.list.d
            state=directory mode=0755'
db01.example.com | success >> {
    "changed": false,
    "gid": 0,
    "group": "root",
    "mode": "0755",
    "owner": "root",
    "path": "/etc/apt/sources.list.d",
    "size": 4096,
    "state": "directory",
    "uid": 0
}
```

The `apt` Module

On Debian and derived distributions, such as Ubuntu, installing and removing packages is generally done with package managers from the apt family, such as apt-get, aptitude, and, in newer versions, the apt binary directly.

The apt module[9] manages this from within Ansible.

```
$ ansible -i myinventory database -m apt \
    -a 'name=screen state=present update_cache=yes'
```

---

[8]http://docs.ansible.com/ansible/file_module.html.
[9]http://docs.ansible.com/ansible/apt_module.html.

```
db01.example.com | success >> {
    "changed": false
}
```

Here, the `screen` package was already installed, so the module didn't change the state of the system.

Separate modules are available for managing apt-keys[10] with which repositories are cryptographically verified and for managing the repositories themselves.[11]

The **yum** and **zypper** Modules

For RPM-based Linux distributions, the yum[12] and zypper modules[13] (at the time of writing, in preview state) are available. They manage package installation via the package managers of the same name.

The **package** Module

The package module[14] uses whatever package manager it detects. It is, thus, more generic than the apt and yum modules but supports far fewer features. For example, in the case of apt, it does not provide any control over whether to run apt-get update before doing anything else.

---

[10]http://docs.ansible.com/ansible/apt_key_module.html.

[11]http://docs.ansible.com/ansible/apt_repository_module.html.

[12]http://docs.ansible.com/ansible/yum_module.html.

[13]http://docs.ansible.com/ansible/zypper_module.html.

[14]http://docs.ansible.com/ansible/package_module.html.

Application-Specific Modules

The modules presented so far are fairly close to the system, but there are also modules for achieving common application-specific tasks. Examples include dealing with databases,[15] network-related things such as proxies,[16] version control systems,[17] clustering solutions such as Kubernetes,[18] and so on.

Playbooks

Playbooks can contain multiple calls to modules in a defined order and limit their execution to individual hosts or group of hosts. They are written in the YAML file format[19], a data serialization file format that is optimized for human readability.

Here is a sample playbook (Listing 7-2) that installs the newest version of the go-agent Debian package, the worker for Go Continuous Delivery (GoCD).[20]

Listing 7-2. An Ansible Playbook for Installing a GoCD Agent on a Debian-Based System

```
---
  - hosts: go-agent
    vars:
      go_server: go-server.example.com
    tasks:
```

---

[15]http://docs.ansible.com/ansible/list_of_database_modules.html.
[16]http://docs.ansible.com/ansible/list_of_network_modules.html.
[17]http://docs.ansible.com/ansible/list_of_source_control_modules.html.
[18]http://docs.ansible.com/ansible/kubernetes_module.html.
[19]http://yaml.org/.
[20]www.gocd.org/.

```
- apt: package=apt-transport-https state=present
- apt_key:
    url: https://download.gocd.org/GOCD-GPG-KEY.asc
    state: present
    validate_certs: no
- apt_repository:
    repo: 'deb https://download.gocd.org /'
    state: present
- apt: update_cache=yes package={{item}} state=present
  with_items:
    - go-agent
    - git
    - build-essential
- lineinfile:
    dest: /etc/default/go-agent
    regexp: ^GO_SERVER=
    line: GO_SERVER={{ go_server }}
- copy:
    src: files/guid.txt
    dest: /var/lib/go-agent/config/guid.txt
    user: go
    group: go
- service: name=go-agent enabled=yes state=started
```

The top-level element in this file is a one-element list. The single element starts with hosts: go-agent, which limits execution to hosts in the group go-agent. This is the relevant part of the inventory file that goes with it:

[go-agent]
```
go-worker01.p6c.org
go-worker02.p6c.org
```

Then it sets the variable go_server to a string, here the hostname where a GoCD server runs.

Finally comes the meat of the playbook: the list of tasks to execute. Each task is a call to a module, some of which have already been discussed. Following is a quick overview.

- First, apt installs the Debian package apt-transport-https, to make sure that the system can fetch metadata and files from Debian repositories through HTTPS.

- The next two tasks use the apt_repository[21] and apt_key[22] modules to configure the repository from which the actual go-agent package will be installed.

- Another call to apt installs the desired package. Also, some more packages are installed with a loop construct.[23]

- The lineinfile module[24] searches by regex (regular expression) for a line in a text file and replaces the line it finds with predefined content. Here, we use that to configure the GoCD server that the agent connects to.

- Finally, the service[25] module starts the agent, if it's not yet running (state=started), and ensures that it is automatically started on reboot (enabled=yes).

Playbooks are invoked with the ansible-playbook command, for example, ansible-playbook -i inventory go-agent.yml.

---

[21]http://docs.ansible.com/ansible/apt_repository_module.html.
[22]http://docs.ansible.com/ansible/apt_key_module.html.
[23]http://docs.ansible.com/ansible/playbooks_loops.html.
[24]http://docs.ansible.com/ansible/lineinfile_module.html.
[25]http://docs.ansible.com/ansible/service_module.html.

There can be more than one list of tasks in a playbook, which is a common use case when they affect different groups of hosts.

```
---
- hosts: go-agent:go-server
  tasks:
    - apt: package=apt-transport-https state=present
    - apt_key:
        url: https://download.gocd.org/GOCD-GPG-KEY.asc
        state: present
        validate_certs: no
    - apt_repository:
        repo: 'deb https://download.gocd.org /'
        state: present

- hosts: go-agent
  tasks:
    - apt: update_cache=yes package={{item}} state=present
      with_items:
        - go-agent
        - git
        - build-essential
    - ...

- hosts: go-server
  tasks:
    - apt: update_cache=yes package={{item}} state=present
    - apt: update_cache=yes package=go-server state=present
    - ...
```

Variables

Variables are useful both for controlling flow inside a playbook and for filling out spots in templates to generate configuration files. There are several ways to set variables. One way is to set them directly in playbooks, via vars: ..., as seen previously. Another is to specify them at the command line.

```
ansible-playbook --extra-vars=variable=value theplaybook.yml
```

A third, very flexible way is to use the group_vars feature. For each group that a host is in, Ansible looks for a file group_vars/thegroup. yml and for files matching group_vars/thegroup/*.yml. A host can be in several groups at once, which gives you extra flexibility.

For example, you can put each host into two groups, one for the role the host is playing (such as web server, database server, DNS server, etc.), and one for the environment it is in (test, staging, prod). Here is a small example that uses this layout.

```
# environments
[prod]
www[01:02].example.com
db01.example.com

[test]
db01.test.example.com
www01.test.example.com

# functional roles
[web]
www[01:02].example.com
www01.test.example.com

[db]
db01.example.com
db01.test.example.com
```

To configure only the test hosts, you can run

```
ansible-playbook --limit test theplaybook.yml
```

and put environment-specific variables in group_vars/test.yml and group_vars/prod.yml and web server–specific variables in group_vars/web.yml, etc.

You can use nested data structures in your variables, and if you do, you can configure Ansible to merge those data structures for you, if they are specified in several sources. You can configure this by creating a file called ansible.cfg, with this content:

[defaults]
```
hash_behavior=merge
```

That way, you can have a file group_vars/all.yml that sets the default values

```
# file group_vars/all.yml
myapp:
    domain: example.com
    db:
        host: db.example.com
        username: myappuser
        instance. myapp
```

and then override individual elements of that nested data structure, for example, in group_vars/test.yml, as follows:

```
# file group_vars/test.yml
myapp:
    domain: test.example.com
    db:
        hostname: db.test.example.com
```

The keys that the `test` group vars file didn't touch, for example, `myapp.db.username`, are inherited from the file `all.yml`.

Roles

Roles are a way to encapsulate parts of a playbook into a reusable component. Let's consider a real-world example that leads to a simple role definition.

For deploying software, you typically want to deploy the exact version just built, so the relevant part of the playbook is

```
- apt:
    name: thepackage={{package_version}}
    state: present
    update_cache: yes
    force: yes
```

But this requires you to supply the `package_version` variable whenever you run the playbook. This will not be practical when you're not running a deployment of a freshly built software, but instead you configure a new machine and have to install several software packages, each with its own playbook.

Hence, we generalize the code to deal with a case in which the version number is absent.

```
- apt:
    name: thepackage={{package_version}}
    state: present
    update_cache: yes
    force: yes
  when: package_version is defined
- apt: name=thepackage state=present update_cache=yes
  when: package_version is undefined
```

If you include several such playbooks in one and run them on the same host, you'll likely notice that it spends most of its time running apt-get update for each included playbook.

Updating the apt cache is necessary the first time, because you might have just uploaded a new package on your local Debian mirror prior to the deployment, but subsequent runs are unnecessary. So, you can store the information that a host has already updated for its cache in a *fact,*[26] which is a kind of per-host variable in Ansible.

```
- apt: update_cache=yes
  when: apt_cache_updated is undefined

- set_fact:
    apt_cache_updated: true
```

As you can see, the code base for sensibly installing a package has grown a bit, and it's time to factor it out into a *role*.

Roles are collections of YAML files with predefined names. The commands

```
$ mkdir roles
$ cd roles
$ ansible-galaxy init custom_package_installation
```

create an empty skeleton for a role named custom_package_installation. The tasks that previously went into all the playbooks now go into the file tasks/main.yml, below the role's main directory (Listing 7-3).

---

[26]https://docs.ansible.com/ansible/set_fact_module.html.

Listing 7-3. File roles/custom_package_installation/tasks/ main.yml

```
- apt: update_cache=yes
  when: apt_cache_updated is undefined
- set_fact:
    apt_cache_updated: true

- apt:
    name: {{package}}={{package_version}}
    state: present
    update_cache: yes
    force: yes
  when: package_version is defined
- apt: name={{package} state=present update_cache=yes
  when: package_version is undefined
```

To use the role, include it in a playbook like this:

```
---
- hosts: web
  pre_tasks:
    - # tasks that are executed before the role(s)
  roles:
    role: custom_package_installation
    package: python-matheval
  tasks:
    - # tasks that are executed after the role(s)
```

pre_tasks and tasks are optional. A playbook consisting only of roles being included is just fine.

Ansible has many more features, such as handlers, that allow you to restart services only once after any changes, dynamic inventories for more flexible server landscapes, Vault for encrypting variables,[27] and a rich ecosystem of existing roles for managing common applications and middleware.

For more about Ansible, I highly recommend the excellent book *Up and Running,* 2nd ed., by Lorin Hochstein (O'Reilly Media, 2017).

7.2 Deploying with Ansible

Armed with knowledge of Ansible from the previous section, deployment becomes a simple task. We start with separate inventory files for the environments (Listing 7-4).

Listing 7-4. Ansible Inventory File `production`

```
[web]
www01.yourorg.com
www02.yourorg.com

[database]
db01.yourorg.com

[all:vars]
ansible_ssh_user=root
```

Perhaps the testing environment requires only a single web server (Listing 7-5).

---

[27]http://docs.ansible.com/ansible/playbooks_vault.html.

Listing 7-5. Ansible Inventory File `testing`

```
[web]
www01.testing.yourorg.com

[database]
db01.stagingyourorg.com

[all:vars]
ansible_ssh_user=root
```

Installing the package `python-matheval` on the web servers in the testing environment is now a one-liner.

```
$ ansible -i testing web -m apt -a 'name=python-matheval
update_cache=yes state=latest'
```

Once you start deploying with Ansible, it's likely you'll want to do other configuration management tasks with it as well, so it makes sense to write a playbook for each package you want to deploy. Here is one (Listing 7-6) using the package installation role from the "Roles" section earlier in this chapter.

Listing 7-6. File `deploy-python-matheval.yml`: Deployment Playbook for Package `python-matheval`

```
---
- hosts: web
  roles:
    role: custom_package_installation
    package: python-matheval
```

You can then invoke it as

```
$ ansible-playbook -i testing deploy-python-matheval.yml
```

7.3 Summary

Ansible can install packages for you, but it can also do much more. It can configure both the operating system and application and even orchestrate processes across several machines.

By writing an inventory file, you tell Ansible which machines it controls. Playbooks specify what to do, using modules to achieve individual tasks, such as creating users or installing software.

CHAPTER 8

A Virtual Playground for Automating Deployments

In the following chapters, we will explore the tool Go continuous delivery (GoCD) and how to package, distribute, and deploy software with it. If you want to follow along and experiment with the things described in these chapters, you will require some machines on which you can do that.

If you don't have the luxury of a public or private cloud in which you can run virtual machines (VMs) and try out the examples, you can use the tools introduced in this chapter to create a playground of VMs on your laptop or workstation. Even if you do have access to a cloud solution, you might want to use some of the scripts presented here, to set up and configure these machines.

8.1 Requirements and Resource Usage

The things we want to do in a virtual playground are

- Build Debian packages.
- Upload them to a local Debian repository.
- Install the packages on one or more servers.

© Moritz Lenz 2019
M. Lenz, *Python Continuous Integration and Delivery*,
https://doi.org/10.1007/978-1-4842-4281-0_8

- Run some lean and simple web services.

- Run deployment and configuration scripts with Ansible.

- Control everything via a GoCD server and agent.

Except for the last task, all of these tasks require very few resources. The GoCD server requires the most resources, with 1GB of RAM minimally and 2GB recommended. The Go server is also the one system that keeps persistent state (such as configuration and pipeline history) that you typically don't want to lose.

So, the easiest approach, and the one I'm taking here, is to install the Go server on the host machine, which is the laptop or workstation that I typically work with.

Then there is one VM for running the Go agent, on which the Debian packages will be built. Two more VMs serve as the target machines on which the freshly built packages will be installed and tested. One of them serves as a testing environment, the second as a production environment.

For those three VMs, the defaults of a half GB of RAM that the tooling provides is quite sufficient. If you use this playground and don't have enough RAM on the host machine, you can try to halve the RAM usage of those VMs. For the target machines, even 200MB might be enough to get started.

8.2 Introducing Vagrant

Vagrant is an abstraction layer over classical virtualization solutions, such as KVM and VirtualBox. It offers base images (called *boxes*) for your VM, manages the VMs for you, and offers a unified API for the initial configuration. It also creates a virtual private network that allows the host machines to talk to the VMs and vice versa.

To install Vagrant, you can download the installer from
`www.vagrantup.com/downloads.html`, or if you use an operating system
with a package manager, such as Debian or RedHat, you can install
it through the package manager. On Debian and Ubuntu, you would
install it with `apt-get install vagrant` (though avoid the 2.0 series
and install 2.1 or newer versions from Vagrant's web site, if only 2.0 is
available through the package manger).

You should also install `virtualbox` in the same way, which acts as a
back end for Vagrant. After you have installed Vagrant, run the following
command:

```
$ vagrant plugin install vagrant-vbguest
```

This installs a Vagrant plug-in that automatically installs *guest tools*
inside Vagrant boxes, which improves configurability and reliability.

To use Vagrant, you write a small Ruby script called `Vagrantfile`,
which instantiates one or more boxes as VMs. You can configure port
forwarding, private or bridged networks, and share directories between the
host and guest VMs.

The `vagrant` command-line tool allows you to create and provision the
VMs with the `vagrant up` command, connect to a VM with `vagrant ssh`,
obtain a status summary with `vagrant status`, and stop and delete the
VMs again with `vagrant destroy`. Calling `vagrant` without any arguments
gives you a summary of the options available.

ℹ   You might wonder why we use Vagrant VMs instead of Docker
containers. The reason is that Docker is optimized to run a single
process or process group. But for our use case, we have to run at
least three processes: the GoCD agent and the application that we
actually want to run there; Aptly, to manage a Debian repository; and
an HTTP server, to allow remote access to the repository.

Network and Vagrant Setup

We'll use Vagrant with a virtual private IP network with addresses from 172.28.128.1 to 172.28.128.254. When you assign one or more addresses of this range to a VM, Vagrant automatically assigns the host machine the address 172.28.128.1.

I've added these lines to my /etc/hosts file. This isn't strictly necessary, but it makes it easier to talk to the VMs.

```
# Vagrant
172.28.128.1 go-server.local
172.28.128.3 testing.local
172.28.128.4 production.local
172.28.128.5 go-agent.local
```

I've also added a few lines to my ~/.ssh/config file.

```
Host 172.28.128.* *.local
    User root
    StrictHostKeyChecking no
    IdentityFile /dev/null
    LogLevel ERROR
```

⚠ **Do not do this for production machines**. This is only safe on a virtual network on a single machine, with which you can be sure that no attacker is present, unless they have already compromised your machine.

Creating and destroying VMs is common in Vagrant land, and each time you create them anew, they will have new host keys. Without such a configuration, you'd spend a lot of time updating SSH key fingerprints.

ℹ️   The Vagrantfile and Ansible playbook introduced here can be found in the deployment-utils repository on GitHub in the playground folder. To follow along, you can use it like this:

```
$ git clone https://github.com/python-ci-cd/
deployment-utils.git

$ cd deployment-utils/playground

$ vagrant up

$ ansible-playbook setup.yml
```

Listing 8-1 shows the Vagrantfile that creates the boxes for the virtual playground.

Listing 8-1. Vagrantfile for the Playground

```
Vagrant.configure(2) do |config|
  config.vm.box = "debian/stretch"

  {
    'testing'     => "172.28.128.3",
    'production'  => "172.28.128.4",
    'go-agent'    => "172.28.128.5",
  }.each do |name, ip|
    config.vm.define name do |instance|
        instance.vm.network "private_network", ip: ip,
            auto_config: false
        instance.vm.hostname = name + '.local'
    end
  end

  config.vm.provision "shell" do |s|
```

```
    ssh_pub_key = File.readlines("#{Dir.home}/.ssh/id_rsa.pub")
        .first.strip
    s.inline = <<-SHELL
      mkdir -p /root/.ssh
      echo #{ssh_pub_key} >> /root/.ssh/authorized_keys
    SHELL
  end
end
```

This Vagrantfile assumes that you have an SSH key pair, and the public key is inside the .ssh/id_rsa.pub path below your home directory, which is the default location for RSA SSH keys on Linux. It uses Vagrant's shell provisioner to add the public key to the authorized_keys file of the root user inside the VMs, so that you can log in via SSH on the guest machines. (Vagrant offers a vagrant ssh command for connecting without this extra step, but I find it easier to use the system ssh command directly, mostly because it is not tied to the presence of the Vagrantfile inside the current working directory.)

In the directory with the Vagrantfile you can then run

```
$ vagrant up
```

to spin up and provision the three VMs. It takes a few minutes when you do it the first time, because Vagrant has to download the base box first.

If everything went fine, you can check that the three VMs are running, by calling vagrant status, as follows:

```
$ vagrant status
Current machine states:

testing                   running (virtualbox)
production                running (virtualbox)
go-agent                  running (virtualbox)
```

This environment represents multiple VMs. The VMs are all
listed above with their current state. For more information
about a specific VM, run `vagrant status NAME`.

And (on Debian-based Linux systems) you should be able to see the
newly created, private network.

```
$ ip route | grep vboxnet
172.28.128.0/24 dev vboxnet1 proto kernel scope link
    src 172.28.128.1
```

Now you can log in to the VMs with ssh root@go-agent.local and
with testing.local and production.local as host names.

8.3 Configuring the Machines

For configuring the VMs, we start with a small ansible.cfg file (Listing 8-2).

Listing 8-2. ansible.cfg: A Configuration File for the Playground

```
[defaults]
host_key_checking = False
inventory = hosts
pipelining=True
```

⚠   Disabling host key checking should only be done in trusted
virtual networks for development systems and never in a production
setting.

The VMs and their IPs are listed in the inventory file (Listing 8-3).

Listing 8-3. hosts Inventory File for the Playground

[all:vars]
```
ansible_ssh_user=root
```

[go-agent]
```
agent.local ansible_ssh_host=172.28.128.5
```

[aptly]
```
go-agent.local
```

[target]
```
testing.local ansible_ssh_host=172.28.128.3
production.local ansible_ssh_host=172.28.128.4
```

[testing]
```
testing.local
```

[production]
```
production.local
```

Then comes the playbook (Listing 8-4), which does all the configuration necessary to run a GoCD agent, an Aptly repository, and SSH access from the go-agent VM to the target VMs.

Listing 8-4. File setup.yml: An Ansible Playbook for Configuring the Three VMs

```
---
 - hosts: go-agent
   vars:
     go_server: 172.28.128.1
   tasks:
   - group: name=go system=yes
   - name: Make sure the go user has an SSH key
```

```
  user: >
      name=go system=yes group=go generate_ssh_key=yes
      home=/var/go
- name: Fetch the ssh public key, so we can distribute it.
  fetch:
      src: /var/go/.ssh/id_rsa.pub
      dest: go-rsa.pub
      fail_on_missing: yes
      flat: yes
- apt: >
      package=apt-transport-https state=present
      update_cache=yes
- apt_key:
      url: https://download.gocd.org/GOCD-GPG-KEY.asc
      state: present
      validate_certs: no
- apt_repository:
      repo: 'deb https://download.gocd.org /'
      state: present
- apt: package={{item}} state=present force=yes
  with_items:
    - openjdk-8-jre-headless
    - go-agent
    - git

- file:
      path: /var/lib/go-agent/config
      state: directory
      owner: go
      group: go
- copy:
      src: files/guid.txt
```

```
        dest: /var/lib/go-agent/config/guid.txt
        owner: go
        group: go
    - name: Go agent configuration for versions 16.8 and above
      lineinfile:
        dest: /etc/default/go-agent
        regexp: ^GO_SERVER_URL=
        line: GO_SERVER_URL=https://{{ go_server }}:8154/go
    - service: name=go-agent enabled=yes state=started

- hosts: aptly
  tasks:
    - apt: package={{item}} state=present
      with_items:
        - ansible
        - aptly
        - build-essential
        - curl
        - devscripts
        - dh-systemd
        - dh-virtualenv
        - gnupg2
        - libjson-perl
        - python-setuptools
        - lighttpd
        - rng-tools
    - copy:
        src: files/key-control-file-gpg2
        dest: /var/go/key-control-file
    - command: killall rngd
      ignore_errors: yes
      changed_when: False
```

```
- command: rngd -r /dev/urandom
  changed_when: False
- command: gpg --gen-key --batch /var/go/key-control-file
  args:
    creates: /var/go/.gnupg/pubring.gpg
  become_user: go
  become: true
  changed_when: False
- shell: gpg --export --armor > /var/go/pubring.asc
  args:
    creates: /var/go/pubring.asc
  become_user: go
  become: true
- fetch:
    src: /var/go/pubring.asc
    dest: deb-key.asc
    fail_on_missing: yes
    flat: yes
- name: Bootstrap aptly repos on the `target` machines
  copy:
    src: ../add-package
    dest: /usr/local/bin/add-package
    mode: 0755
- name: Download an example package to fill the repo with
  get_url:
    url: https://perlgeek.de/static/dummy.deb
    dest: /tmp/dummy.deb
- command: >
      /usr/local/bin/add-package {{item}}
      stretch /tmp/dummy.deb
  with_items:
```

```
          - testing
          - production
      become_user: go
      become: true
    - user: name=www-data groups=go

    - name: Configure lighttpd to serve the aptly directories
      copy:
          src: files/lighttpd.conf
          dest: /etc/lighttpd/conf-enabled/30-aptly.conf
    - service: name=lighttpd state=restarted enabled=yes

- hosts: target
  tasks:
    - authorized_key:
      user: root
      key: "{{ lookup('file', 'go-rsa.pub') }}"
    - apt_key:
          data: "{{ lookup('file', 'deb-key.asc') }}"
          state: present

- hosts: production
  tasks:
    - apt_repository:
      repo: >
          deb http://172.28.128.5/debian/production/stretch
          stretch main
      state: present

- hosts: testing
  tasks:
    - apt_repository:
      repo:
          deb http://172.28.128.5/debian/testing/stretch
```

```
        stretch main
      state: present

- hosts: go-agent
  tasks:
    - name: 'Checking SSH connectivity to {{item}}'
      become: True
      become_user: go
      command: >
        ssh -o StrictHostkeyChecking=No
        root@"{{ hostvars[item]['ansible_ssh_host'] }}" true
      changed_when: false
      with_items:
          - testing.local
          - production.local
```

This does a lot of stuff. It

- Installs and configures the GoCD agent

  - It copies a file with a fixed UID to the configuration
    directory of the Go agent, so that when you tear
    down the machine and create it anew, the Go
    server will identify it as the same agent as before.

- Gives the go user on the go-agent machine SSH access
  on the target hosts by

  - First making sure the Go user has an SSH key

  - Copying the public SSH key to the host machine

  - Later distributing it to the target machines using
    the authorized_key module

- Creates a GPG key pair for the go user

    - Because GPG key creation uses lots of entropy for random numbers, and VMs typically don't have that much entropy, it first installs rng-tools and uses that to convince the system to use lower-quality randomness. Again, this is something you should never do in a production setting.

- Copies the public key of said GPG key pair to the host machine and distributes it to the target machines using the apt_key module

- Creates some Aptly-based Debian repositories on the go-agent machine by

    - Copying the add-package script from the same repository to the go-agent machine

    - Running it with a dummy package to actually create the repositories

    - Installing and configuring lighttpd to serve these packages over HTTP

    - Configuring the target machines to use these repositories as a package source

- Checks that the Go user on the go-agent machine can indeed reach the other VMs via SSH

After running the playbook with ansible-playbook setup.yml, you have a GoCD agent waiting to connect to a server. Installing a GoCD server is covered in the next chapter. After installing the GoCD server, you have to activate the agent in the web configuration and assign the appropriate resources (debian-stretch, build, and aptly, if you follow the examples from this book).

8.4 Summary

Vagrant helps you to set up a virtual playground for CD by managing VMs and a private network. We have seen an Ansible playbook that configures these machines to provide all the infrastructure you need to run a GoCD server on the host machine.

CHAPTER 9

Building in the Pipeline with Go Continuous Delivery

The previous chapters have demonstrated the automation of the essential steps from source code to deployment: build, distribution, and deployment. What's missing now is the glue that holds them all together: polling the source code repositories, getting packages from the build server to the repository server and generally controlling the flow, aborting the pipeline instance when one step has failed, and so on.

We will use Go Continuous Delivery[1] (GoCD or Go) by ThoughtWorks as glue.

9.1 About Go Continuous Delivery

GoCD is an open source project written in Java, with components of its web interface in Ruby on Rails. It started out as proprietary software in 2010 and was open sourced in 2014.

---

[1] www.gocd.org/.

You can download GoCD for Windows, OSX, Debian and RPM-based Linux distributions, and Solaris. Commercial support for GoCD is available from ThoughtWorks.

It consists of a server component that holds the pipeline configuration, polls source code repositories for changes, schedules and distributes work, collects artifacts, presents a web interface to visualize and control it all, and offers a mechanism for manual approval of steps.

One or more *agents* connect to the server and carry out the actual jobs in the build pipeline.

Pipeline Organization

Every build, deployment, or test job that GoCD executes must be part of a *pipeline*. A pipeline consists of one or more linearly arranged *stages*. Within a stage, one or more *jobs* run potentially in parallel and are individually distributed to agents. *Tasks* are serially executed within a job.

In a task, you can rely on files that previous tasks in the same job produced, whereas between jobs and stages, you have to explicitly capture and later retrieve them as artifacts. More on that follows.

The most general task is the execution of an external program. Other tasks include the retrieval of artifacts or language-specific things such as running Ant or Rake builds.[2]

Pipelines can trigger other pipelines, allowing you to form an acyclic, directed graph of pipelines (Figure 9-1).

---

[2]The <ant> and <rake> tasks execute the specialized builders of the same name and allow you to specify targets and build files. See https://docs.gocd.org/ current/configuration/configuration_reference.html#ant for more information.

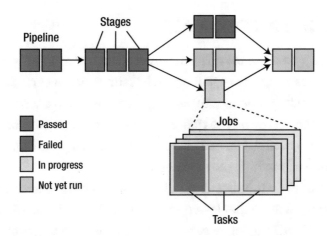

Figure 9-1. *GoCD pipelines can form a graph. Pipelines consist of sequential stages in which several jobs can run in parallel. Tasks are serially executed inside a job.*

Matching of Jobs to Agents

When an agent is idle, it polls the server for work. If the server has jobs to run, it uses two criteria to decide if the agent is fit for carrying out the job: *environments* and *resources*.

Each job is part of a pipeline, and if you choose to use environments, a pipeline is part of an environment. On the other hand, each agent is configured to be part of one or more environments. An agent only accepts jobs from pipelines from one of its environments.

Resources are user-defined labels that describe what an agent has to offer, and inside a pipeline configuration, you can specify what resources a job requires. For example, if you define that a job requires the phantomjs resource to test a web application, only agents that you assign this resource to will execute that job. It is a good idea to add the operating system and version as resources. In the preceding example, the agent might have the phantomjs, debian, and debian-stretch resources, offering the author of the job some choice of granularity for specifying the required operating system.

A Word on Environments

GoCD makes it possible to run agents in specific environments. As an example, one can run a Go agent on each testing and on each production machine and match pipelines to agent environments, to ensure that an installation step occurs on the right machine in the right environment. If you go with this model, you can also use GoCD to copy the build artifacts to the machines for which they are needed.

I chose not to do this, because I didn't want to have to install a GoCD agent on each machine that I want to deploy to. Instead, I use Ansible, executed on a GoCD agent, to control all machines in an environment. This requires managing the SSH keys that Ansible uses and distributing packages through a Debian repository. But because Debian requires a repository anyway, to be able to resolve dependencies, this is not much of an extra burden.

Materials

A *material* in GoCD serves two purposes: it triggers a pipeline, and it provides files that the tasks in the pipeline can work with.

I tend to use Git repositories as materials, and GoCD can poll these repositories, triggering the pipeline when a new version becomes available. The GoCD agent also clones the repositories into the file system in which the agent executes its jobs.

There are material plug-ins for various source control systems, such as Subversion (svn) and mercurial, and plug-ins for treating Debian and RPM package repositories as materials.

Finally, a pipeline can serve as a material for other pipelines. Using this feature, you can build graphs of pipelines.

Artifacts

GoCD can collect *artifacts*, which are files or directories generated by a job. Later parts of the same pipeline, or even of other, connected pipelines, can retrieve those artifacts. Retrieval of artifacts is not limited to artifacts created on the same agent machine.

You can also retrieve artifacts from the web interface and from a REST API that the GoCD server provides.[3]

The artifact repository can be configured to discard older versions when disk space becomes scarce.

9.2 Installation

In order to use GoCD, you have to install the GoCD server on one machine and a GoCD agent on at least one machine. This can be on the same machine as the server or on a different one, as long as it can connect to the GoCD server with ports 8153 and 8154.

When your infrastructure and the number of pipelines grow, it is likely that you will be running several Go agents.

Installing the GoCD Server on Debian

To install the GoCD server on a Debian-based operating system, first you have to make sure you can download Debian packages via HTTPS.

```
$ apt-get install -y apt-transport-https
```

---

[3]https://api.gocd.org/current/.

Then you have to configure the package sources.

```
$ echo 'deb https://download.gocd.org /' \
        > /etc/apt/sources.list.d/gocd.list
$ curl https://download.gocd.org/GOCD-GPG-KEY.asc \
        | apt-key add -
```

And finally install it.

```
$ apt-get update && apt-get install -y go-server
```

On Debian 9, codename *Stretch*, Java 8 is available out of the box. In older versions of Debian, you might have to install Java 8 from other sources, such as Debian Backports.[4]

When you now point your browser at port 8154 of the Go server for HTTPS (ignore the SSL security warnings), or port 8153 for HTTP, you should see the GoCD server's web interface (Figure 9-2).

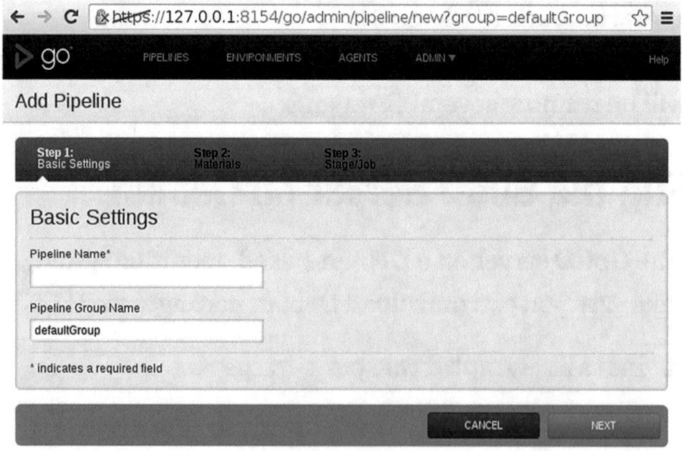

Figure 9-2. *GoCD's initial web interface*

---

[4]https://backports.debian.org/.

If you get a *connection refused* error, check the files under /var/log/ go-server/ for hints of what went wrong.

To prevent unauthenticated access, you can install authentication plug-ins, for example, password file-based authentication[5] or LDAP or Active Directory–based authentication.[6]

Installing a GoCD Agent on Debian

On one or more machines on which you want to execute the automated build and deployment steps, you must install a Go agent, which will connect to the server and poll it for work.

See Chapter 8 for an example of automatic installation of a GoCD agent. If you want to do it manually instead, you must perform the same first three steps as when installing the GoCD server, to ensure that you can install packages from the GoCD package repository. Then, of course, you install the Go agent. On a Debian-based system, this is the following:

```
$ apt-get install -y apt-transport-https
$ echo 'deb https://download.gocd.org /' >
    /etc/apt/sources.list.d/gocd.list
$ curl https://download.gocd.org/GOCD-GPG-KEY.asc \
    | apt-key add -
$ apt-get update && apt-get install -y go-agent
```

Then edit the file /etd/default/go-agent. The first line should read

```
GO_SERVER_URL=https://127.0.0.1:8154/go
```

---

[5]https://github.com/gocd/gocd-filebased-authentication-plugin.
[6]https://github.com/gocd/gocd-ldap-authentication-plugin.

Change the variable to point to your GoCD server machine, then start the agent.

```
$ service go-agent start
```

After a few seconds, the agent will have contacted the server. When you click the Agents menu in the GoCD server's web interface, you should see the agent (Figure 9-3).

Figure 9-3. *Screenshot of GoCD's agent management interface. (*lara *is the host name of the agent here.)*

First Contact with GoCD's XML Configuration

There are two ways to configure your GoCD server: through the web interface and through a configuration file in XML. You can also edit the XML config through the web interface.[7]

While the web interface is a good way to explore GoCD's capabilities, it quickly becomes annoying to use, due to too much clicking. Using an editor with good XML support gets things done much faster, and it lends itself better to compact explanation, so that's the route I'm taking here. You can also use both approaches on the same GoCD server instance.

---

[7]Starting from GoCD version 16.7, pipeline configurations can be swapped out to external version control repositories and, through plug-ins, can even be written in different formats, such as YAML. While this seems like a very promising approach, introducing it is outside the scope of this book.

In the Admin menu, the Config XML item lets you see and edit the server config. Listing 9-1 is what a pristine XML configuration looks like, with one agent already registered.

Listing 9-1. Baseline GoCD XML Configuration, with One Agent Registered

```
<?xml version="1.0" encoding="utf-8"?>
<cruise
    xmlns:xsi="http://www.w3.org/2001/XMLSchema-instance"
    xsi:noNamespaceSchemaLocation="cruise-config.xsd"
    schemaVersion="77">
<server artifactsdir="artifacts"
        commandRepositoryLocation="default"
        serverId="b2ce4653-b333-4b74-8ee6-8670be479df9">
</server>
<agents>
    <agent hostname="lara" ipaddress="192.168.2.43"
        uuid="19e70088-927f-49cc-980f-2b1002048e09" />
</agents>
</cruise>
```

The serverId and the data of the agent will differ in your installation, even if you followed the same steps.

To give the agent some resources, you can change the <agent .../> tag in the <agents> section to read as shown in Listing 9-2.

Listing 9-2. GoCD XML Configuration for an Agent with Resources

```
<agent hostname="lara" ipaddress="192.168.2.43"
    uuid="19e70088-927f-49cc-980f-2b1002048e09">
  <resources>
    <resource>debian-stretch</resource>
```

```
    <resource>build</resource>
    <resource>aptly</resource>
  </resources>
</agent>
```

Creating an SSH Key

It is convenient for GoCD to have an SSH key without a password, to be able to clone Git repositories via SSH, for example. To create one, run the following commands on the server:

```
$ su - go
$ ssh-keygen -t rsa -b 2048 -N " -f ~/.ssh/id_rsa
```

Either copy the resulting .ssh directory and the files therein onto each agent into the /var/go directory (and remember to set owner and permissions as they were created originally) or create a new key pair on each agent.

9.3 Building in the Pipeline

Triggering the build of a Debian package requires fetching the source code from a Git repository, by configuring it as a GoCD material, then invoking the dpkg-buildpackage command with some options, and, finally, collecting the resulting files.

Here (Listing 9-3) is the first shot at building the python-matheval package, expressed in GoCD's XML configuration.

Listing 9-3. Simple Approach to Building a Debian Package in GoCD

```
<pipelines group="deployment">
  <pipeline name="python-matheval">
    <materials>
      <git
url="https://github.com/python-ci-cd/python-matheval.git"
        dest="source" />
    </materials>
    <stage name="build" cleanWorkingDir="true">
      <jobs>
        <job name="build-deb" timeout="5">
          <tasks>
            <exec command="/bin/bash" workingdir="source">
              <arg>-c</arg>
              <arg>dpkg-buildpackage -b -us -uc</arg>
            </exec>
          </tasks>
          <artifacts>
            <artifact src="*.deb" dest="debian-packages/"
                type="build" />
          </artifacts>
          <resources>
            <resource>debian-stretch</resource>
            <resource>build</resource>
          </resources>
        </job>
      </jobs>
    </stage>
  </pipeline>
</pipelines>
```

You can find this and all following XML configurations in the gocd directory of the deployment-utils[8] repository.

The outermost tag is a pipeline group, which has a name. It can be used to categorize available pipelines and also to manage permissions.

The second level is the <pipeline> with a name, and it contains a list of materials and one or more stages.

Directory Layout

Each time a job within a stage is run, the GoCD agent that is assigned to the job prepares a directory in which it makes the materials available. On Linux, this directory defaults to /var/lib/go-agent/pipelines/, followed by the pipeline name. Paths in the GoCD configuration are relative to this path.

For example, the preceding material definition contains the attribute dest="source", so the absolute path to this Git repository's working copy is /var/lib/go-agent/pipelines/python-matheval/source. Leaving out the dest="..." would work and give one less directory level, but it would also prevent us from using a second material in the future.

See the config references[9] for a list of available material types and options. Plug-ins are available[10] that add further material types.

Stages, Jobs, Tasks, and Artifacts

All the stages in a pipeline run serially, and each one runs only if the previous stage succeeded. Each stage has a name, which is used both in the front end and for fetching artifacts produced in that stage.

---

[8]https://github.com/python-ci-cd/deployment-utils.

[9]https://docs.gocd.org/current/configuration/configuration_reference.
html#materials.

[10]www.gocd.org/plugins/.

In the preceding example, I gave the stage the attribute `cleanWorkingDir="true"`, which makes GoCD delete files created during the previous build and discard changes to files under version control. This tends to be a good option to use; otherwise, you might unknowingly slide into a situation in which a previous build affects the current build, which can be really painful to debug.

Jobs are potentially executed in parallel within a stage and have names for the same reasons that stages do. The jobs only run in parallel if several agents are available to run them.

The GoCD agent serially executes the tasks within a job. I tend to mostly use `<exec>` tasks (and `<fetchartifact>`, which you will see in the next chapter), which invoke system commands. They follow the UNIX convention of treating an exit status of zero as success and everything else as a failure.

For more complex commands, I create shell, Perl, or Python scripts inside a Git repository and add the repository as a material to the pipeline, which makes them available during the build process, with no extra effort.

The `<exec>` task in our example invokes `/bin/bash -c 'dpkg-buildpackage -b -us -uc'`. This is a case of Cargo Cult Programming,[11] because invoking `dpkg-buildpackage` directly works just as well. Ah well, we can revise this later...

`dpkg-buildpackage -b -us -uc` builds the Debian package and is executed inside the Git checkout of the source. It produces a `.deb` file, a `.changes` file, and possibly a few other files with metadata. They are created one level above the Git checkout, in the root directory of the pipeline.

---

[11]Wikipedia, "Cargo cult programming," https://en.wikipedia.org/wiki/Cargo_cult_programming, 2018.

Because these are the files that we want to work with later on, at least the .deb file, we let GoCD store them in an internal database called the *artifact repository*. That's what the <artifact> tag in the configuration instructs GoCD to do.

The name of the generated package files depend on the version number of the built Debian package (which comes from the debian/ changelog file in the Git repository), so it's not easy to reference them by name later on. That's where the dest="debian-packages/" comes into play: it makes GoCD store the artifacts in a directory with a fixed name. Later stages then can retrieve all artifact files from this directory by the fixed directory name.

The Pipeline in Action

If nothing goes wrong (and nothing ever does, right?), Figure 9-4 shows roughly what the web interface looks like after running the new pipeline.

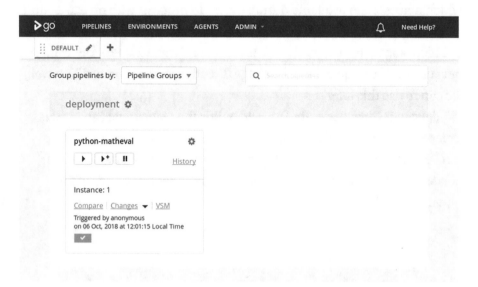

Figure 9-4. *Pipeline overview after a successful run of the build stage*

Whenever there is a new commit in the Git repository, GoCD happily builds a Debian package and stores it for further use. Automated builds, yay!

Version Recycling Considered Harmful

When building a Debian package, the tooling determines the version number of the resulting package, by looking at the top of the debian/ changelog file. This means that whenever somebody pushes code or documentation changes without a new changelog entry, the resulting Debian package has the same version number as the previous one.

Most Debian tooling assumes that the tuple of package name, version, and architecture uniquely identifies a revision of a package. Stuffing a new version of a package with an old version number into a repository is bound to cause trouble. Most repository-management software simply refuses to accept a copy of a package that recycles a version. On the target machine on which the package is to be installed, upgrading the package won't do anything, if the version number stays the same.

Constructing Unique Version Numbers

There are several sources that you can tap to generate unique version numbers.

- Randomness (for example, in the form of UUIDs)
- The current date and time
- The Git repository itself
- Several environment variables[12] that GoCD exposes that can be of use

---

[12]https://docs.gocd.org/current/faq/dev_use_current_revision_in_build.html.

The latter is promising. GO_PIPELINE_COUNTER is a monotonic counter that increases each time GoCD runs the pipeline, so a good source for a version number. GoCD allows manual rerunning of stages, so it's best to combine it with GO_STAGE_COUNTER. In terms of shell scripting, using $GO_PIPELINE_COUNTER.$GO_STAGE_COUNTER as a version string sounds like a decent approach.

But, there's more. GoCD allows you to trigger a pipeline with a specific version of a material, so you can have a new pipeline run to build an old version of the software. If you do that, using GO_PIPELINE_COUNTER as the first part of the version string doesn't reflect the use of the old code base.

git describe is an established way to count commits. By default, it prints the last tag in the repository, and if HEAD does not resolve to the same commit as the tag, it adds the number of commits since that tag and the abbreviated SHA1 hash prefixed by g, so, for example, 2016.04-32-g4232204 for the commit 4232204, which is 32 commits after the tag 2016.04. The option --long forces it to always print the number of commits and the hash, even when HEAD points to a tag.

We don't need the commit hash for the version number, so a shell script to construct a suitable version number looks like this.

```
#!/bin/bash
set -e
set -o pipefail
v=$(git describe --long |sed 's/-g[A-Fa-f0-9]*$//')
version="$v.${GO_PIPELINE_COUNTER:-0}.${GO_STAGE_COUNTER:-0}"
```

Bash's ${VARIABLE:-default} syntax is a good way to make the script work outside a GoCD agent environment. This script requires a tag to be set in the Git repository. If there is none, it fails with this message from git describe:

```
fatal: No names found, cannot describe anything.
```

Other Bits and Pieces Around the Build

Now that we have a unique version string, we must instruct the build
system to use this version string. This works by writing a new entry in
debian/changelog with the desired version number. The debchange tool
automates this for us. A few options are necessary to make it work reliably.

```
export DEBFULLNAME='Go Debian Build Agent'
export DEBEMAIL='go-noreply@example.com'
debchange --newversion=$version --force-distribution -b \
    --distribution="${DISTRIBUTION:-stretch}" 'New Version'
```

When we want to reference this version number in later stages in the
pipeline (yes, there will be more), it's handy to have it available in a file.
It is also handy to have it in the output, so we need two more lines in the
script.

```
echo $version
echo $version > ../version
```

and ,of course, must trigger the actual build, as follows:

```
dpkg-buildpackage -b -us -uc
```

Plugging It into GoCD

To make the script accessible to GoCD, and also have it under version
control, I put the script into a Git repository, under the name debian-
autobuild, and added the repository as a material to the pipeline
(Listing 9-4).

Listing 9-4. GoCD Configuration for Building Packages with
Distinct Version Numbers

```
<pipeline name="python-matheval">
  <materials>
    <git
url="https://github.com/python-ci-cd/python-matheval.git"
        dest="source" materialName="python-matheval" />
    <git
url="https://github.com/python-ci-cd/deployment-utils.git"
      dest="deployment-utils" materialName="deployment-utils" />
  </materials>
  <stage name="build" cleanWorkingDir="true">
    <jobs>
      <job name="build-deb" timeout="5">
        <tasks>
          <exec command="../deployment-utils/debian-autobuild"
                workingdir="source" />
        </tasks>
        <artifacts>
          <artifact src="version" type="build"/>
          <artifact src="*.deb" dest="debian-packages/"
            type="build" />
        </artifacts>
        <resources>
          <resource>debian-stretch</resource>
          <resource>build</resource>
        </resources>
      </job>
    </jobs>
  </stage>
</pipeline>
```

Now, GoCD automatically builds Debian packages on each commit to the Git repository and gives each a distinct version string.

9.4 Summary

GoCD is an open source tool that can poll your Git repositories and trigger the build through dedicated agents. It is configured through a web interface, either by clicking through assistants or providing an XML configuration.

Care must be taken to construct meaningful version numbers for each build. Git tags, the number of commits since the last tag, and counters exposed by GoCD are useful components with which to construct such version numbers.

## CHAPTER 10

Distributing and Deploying Packages in the Pipeline

The previous chapter has left us with the beginning of a GoCD pipeline. It automatically builds a Debian package each time new commits are pushed to Git and generates a unique version number for each build. Finally, it captures as artifacts the built package and a file called version containing the version number. The next tasks are to upload it into a Debian repository and deploy it on the target machines.

10.1 Uploading in the Pipeline

Chapter 6, on distributing packages, already introduced a small program for creating and filling Debian repositories managed with Aptly. If you add it to the deployment-utils Git repository from that chapter, you can automatically upload the newly built packages with this additional GoCD configuration (Listing 10-1), to be inserted after the build stage.

© Moritz Lenz 2019
M. Lenz, *Python Continuous Integration and Delivery*,
https://doi.org/10.1007/978-1-4842-4281-0_10

Listing 10-1. GoCD Configuration for Uploading a Freshly Built Package to the `testing` Repository

```
<stage name="upload-testing">
  <jobs>
    <job name="upload-testing">
      <tasks>
        <fetchartifact pipeline="" stage="build"
            job="build-deb" srcdir="debian-packages"
            artifactOrigin="gocd">
          <runif status="passed" />
        </fetchartifact>
        <exec command="/bin/bash">
          <arg>-c</arg>
      <arg>deployment-utils/add-package testing stretch *.deb</arg>
        </exec>
      </tasks>
      <resources>
        <resource>aptly</resource>
      </resources>
    </job>
  </jobs>
</stage>
```

The `fetchartifact` task fetches, you guessed it, an artifact that is stored in the GoCD server's artifact repository. Here, it fetches the directory `python-matheval`, into which the previous stage uploaded the Debian package. The empty string for the pipeline name instructs GoCD to use the current pipeline.

In the invocation of the `add-package` script, `testing` refers to the name of the environment (which you can choose freely, as long as you are consistent), not the testing distribution of the Debian project.

Finally, the `aptly` resource selects a GoCD agent with the same resource to run the job on (see Figure 10-1). If you anticipate that your setup will grow a bit, you should have a separate machine for serving these repositories. Install a GoCD agent on it and assign it this resource. You can even have separate machines for the testing and production repositories and give them more specific resources (such as `aptly-testing` and `aptly-production`).

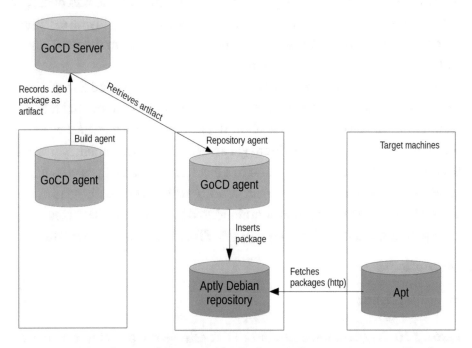

Figure 10-1. *The machine on which the Aptly repository resides has a GoCD agent that retrieves the Debian packages as artifacts from the GoCD server. Target machines configure the repository as a package source.*

User Accounts and Security

In the previous sample configuration, the add-package script runs as the go system user, whose home directory on Linux-based systems is /var/go by default. This will create repositories in a directory such as /var/go/aptly/testing/stretch/.

In Chapter 6, the assumption was that Aptly runs under its own system user account. You still have to give the go user permissions to add packages to the repository, but you can prevent the go user from modifying existing repositories and, more important, from getting access from the GPG key with which the packages are signed.

If you keep the repository under a separate user, you need a way to cross the user account barrier, and the traditional way to do that for command-line applications is to allow the go user to call add-package through the sudo command. But to get an actual security benefit, you have to copy the add-package command to a location where the go user has no write permissions. Otherwise, an attacker with access to the go user account could just modify this command to do whatever he/she sees fit.

Assuming you intend to copy it to /usr/local/bin, you can add this line:

/etc/sudoers

to the file (Listing 10-2).

Listing 10-2. /etc/sudoers Line That Allows the go User to Execute add-package As User aptly

```
go ALL=(aptly) NOPASSWD: /usr/local/bin/add-package
```

Then, instead of calling add-package <environment> <distribution> <deb package>, you change it to

```
$ sudo -u aptly --set-home /usr/local/bin/add-package \
    <environment> <distribution> <deb package>
```

The --set-home flags tells sudo to set the HOME environment variable to the home directory of the target user, here aptly.

If you choose not to go the sudo route, you have to adapt the web server configuration to serve files from /var/go/aptly/ instead of /home/aptly/aptly.

10.2 Deploying in the Pipeline

In Chapter 7, we saw how to upgrade (or install, if it's not yet installed) a package through Ansible (see Figure 10-2), as follows:

```
$ ansible -i testing web -m apt \
    -a 'name=python-matheval state=latest update_cache=yes'
```

where testing is the inventory file of the same name as the environment, web is the group of hosts to deploy to, and python-matheval is the name of the package.

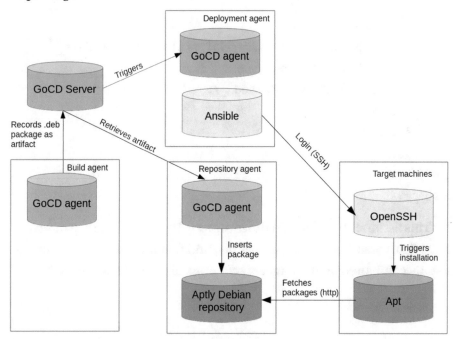

Figure 10-2. *The GoCD agent runs Ansible to connect to the target machines via SSH, to install the desired package*

147

You can do this in GoCD as a separate stage, after the `upload-testing` stage (Listing 10-3).

Listing 10-3. GoCD Configuration for Automatically Installing a Package

```
<stage name="deploy-testing">
  <jobs>
    <job name="deploy-testing">
      <tasks>
        <exec command="ansible" workingdir="deployment-utils/
        ansible/">
          <arg>--inventory-file=testing</arg>
          <arg>web</arg>
          <arg>-m</arg>
          <arg>apt</arg>
          <arg>-a</arg>
          <arg>name=python-matheval state=latest update_
          cache=yes</arg>
          <runif status="passed" />
        </exec>
      </tasks>
    </job>
  </jobs>
</stage>
```

This assumes that you add the inventory files in the `ansible` directory of the `deployment-utils` Git repository, and that the Debian repository is already configured on the target machine, as discussed in Chapter 7.

10.3 Results

To run the new stage, either trigger a complete run of the pipeline by hitting the "play" triangle in the pipeline overview on the web front end or do a manual trigger of that one stage in the pipe history view. You can log in on the target machine, to check if the package was successfully installed.

```
$ dpkg -l python-matheval
Desired=Unknown/Install/Remove/Purge/Hold
| Status=Not/Inst/Conf-files/Unpacked/halF-conf/Half-inst/
|/ Err?=(none)/Reinst-required (Status,Err: uppercase=bad)
||/ Name            Version      Architecture Description
+++-==============-============-============-===============
ii python-matheval 0.1-0.7.1    all          Web service
```

and verify that the service is running

```
$ systemctl status python-matheval
  python-matheval.service - Package installation informati
    Loaded: loaded (/lib/systemd/system/python-matheval.ser
    Active: active (running) since Sun 2016-03-27 13:15:41
   Process: 4439 ExecStop=/usr/bin/hypnotoad -s /usr/lib/py
  Main PID: 4442 (/usr/lib/packag)
    CGroup: /system.slice/python-matheval.service
            ├─4442 /usr/lib/python-matheval/python-matheval
            ├─4445 /usr/lib/python-matheval/python-matheval
            ├─4446 /usr/lib/python-matheval/python-matheval
            ├─4447 /usr/lib/python-matheval/python-matheval
            └─4448 /usr/lib/python-matheval/python-matheval
```

You can also check from the host machine that the service responds on port 8080, as it's supposed to.

```
$ curl --data '["+", 5]' -XPOST http://172.28.128.3:8800
5
```

10.4 Going All the Way to Production

Uploading and deploying to production works the same as with the testing environment. So, all that's required is to duplicate the configuration of the last two pipelines, replace every occurrence of testing with production, and add a manual approval button, so that production deployment remains a conscious decision (Listing 10-4).

Listing 10-4. GoCD Configuration for Distributing in, and Deploying to, the Production Environment

```
<stage name="upload-production">
  <approval type="manual" />
  <jobs>
    <job name="upload-production">
      <tasks>
        <fetchartifact pipeline="" stage="build" job="build-
        deb" srcdir="debian-packages" artifactOrigin="gocd">
          <runif status="passed" />
        </fetchartifact>
        <exec command="/bin/bash">
          <arg>-c</arg>
          <arg>deployment-utils/add-package production \
               stretch *.deb</arg>
        </exec>
      </tasks>
      <resources>
        <resource>aptly</resource>
      </resources>
    </job>
  </jobs>
</stage>
```

```
<stage name="deploy-production">
  <jobs>
    <job name="deploy-production">
      <tasks>
        <exec command="ansible" workingdir="deployment-utils/
                      ansible/">
          <arg>--inventory-file=production</arg>
          <arg>web</arg>
          <arg>-m</arg>
          <arg>apt</arg>
          <arg>-a</arg>
      <arg>name=python-matheval state=latest update_cache=yes</arg>
          <runif status="passed" />
        </exec>
      </tasks>
    </job>
  </jobs>
</stage>
```

The only real news here is the second line

```
<approval type="manual" />
```

which makes GoCD proceed to this stage only when someone clicks the approval arrow in the web interface.

You also must fill out the inventory file called production with the list of your server or servers.

10.5 Achievement Unlocked: Basic Continuous Delivery

To recapitulate, the pipeline

- Is triggered automatically from commits in the source code

- Automatically builds a Debian package from each commit

- Uploads it to a repository for the testing environment

- Automatically installs it in the testing environment

- Uploads it, upon manual approval, to a repository for the production environment

- Automatically installs the new version in production

The basic framework for automated deployments from a Git commit in the sources to software running in production is now in place.

## CHAPTER 11

Pipeline Improvements

The pipeline from the previous chapter is already quite usable and vastly preferable to manual builds, distribution, and installation. That said, there is room for improvement. I will discuss how to change it to always deploy the exact version that was built in the same instance of the pipeline, how to run smoke tests after installation, and how to extract a template from the Go continuous delivery (GoCD) configuration, so that it becomes easily reusable.

11.1 Rollbacks and Installing Specific Versions

The deployment pipeline developed in the previous chapters always installs the latest version of a package. Because the logic for constructing version numbers usually produces monotonously increasing version numbers, this is usually the package that was built previously in the same pipeline instance.

However, we really want the pipeline to deploy the exact version that was built inside the same instance of the pipeline. The obvious benefit is that it allows you to rerun older versions of the pipeline, to install older versions, effectively giving you a rollback.

© Moritz Lenz 2019
M. Lenz, *Python Continuous Integration and Delivery*,
https://doi.org/10.1007/978-1-4842-4281-0_11

Alternatively, you can build a second pipeline for hotfixes, based on the same Git repository but a different branch. When you want a hotfix, you simply pause the regular pipeline and trigger the hotfix pipeline. In this scenario, if you always installed the newest version, finding a proper version string for the hotfix would be nearly impossible, because it must be higher than the currently installed one but also lower than the next regular build. Oh, and all of that automatically, please.

A less obvious benefit to installing a very specific version is that it detects errors in the package source configuration of the target machines. If the deployment script only installs the newest version that's available, and through an error the repository isn't configured on the target machine, the installation process becomes a silent no-op, if the package is already installed in an older version.

Implementation

There are two things to do: figure out which version of the package to install, and then do it. How to install a specific version of a package with Ansible (Listing 11-1) has already been explained in Chapter 7.

Listing 11-1. Ansible Playbook Fragment for Installing Version 1.00 of Package foo

```
- apt: name=foo=1.00 state=present force=yes
```

The more generic way is to use the role custom_package_installation covered in the same chapter.

```
- hosts: web roles:
  role: custom_package_installation
  package: python-matheval
```

You can invoke this with ansible-playbook --extra-vars=package_version=1.00....

Add this playbook to the `deployment-utils` Git repository as file `ansible/deploy-python-matheval.yml`. Finding the version number to install also has a simple, though perhaps not obvious, solution: write the version number to a file; collect this file as an artifact in GoCD; and then, when it's time to install, fetch the artifact and read the version number from it. At the time of writing, GoCD does not have a more direct way to propagate metadata through pipelines.

The GoCD configuration for passing the version to the Ansible playbook looks like Listing 11-2.

Listing 11-2. GoCD Configuration for Installing the Version from the `version` File

```
<job name="deploy-testing">
  <tasks>
    <fetchartifact pipeline="" stage="build" job="build-deb"
         srcfile="version" artifactOrigin="gocd" />
    <exec command="/bin/bash" workingdir="deployment-utils/
         ansible/">
      <arg>-c</arg>
      <arg>ansible-playbook --inventory-file=testing
--extra-vars="package_version=$(&lt; ../../version)" deploy-
         python-matheval.yml</arg>
    </exec>
  </tasks>
</job>
```

(The `<arg>...</arg>` XML tag must be on one line, so that Bash interprets it as a single command. It is shown here on multiple lines merely for readability.)

Bash's `$(...)` opens a subprocess, which, again, is a Bash process, and inserts the output from that subprocess into the command line. `< ../../version` is a short way of reading the file, and this being XML, the less-than sign needs to be escaped.

The production deployment configuration looks pretty much the same, just with `--inventory-file=production`.

Try It!

To test the version-specific package installation, you must have at least two runs of the pipeline that captured the `version` artifact. If you don't have that yet, you can push commits to the source repository, and GoCD picks them up automatically.

You can query the installed version on the target machine with `dpkg -l python-matheval`. After the last run, the version built in that pipeline instance should be installed.

Then you can rerun the deployment stage from a previous pipeline, for example, in the history view of the pipeline, by hovering with the mouse over the stage and then clicking the circle with the arrow on it that triggers the rerun (Figure 11-1).

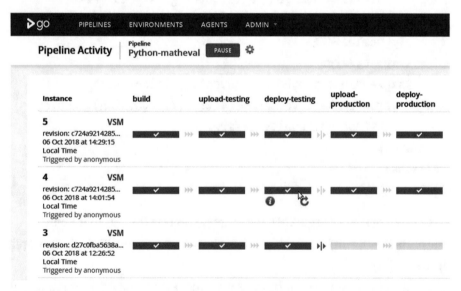

Figure 11-1. *In the history view of a pipeline, hovering over a complete stage (passed or failed) gives you an icon for rerunning the stage*

When the stage has finished running, you can again check the installed version of the package on the target machine, to verify that the older version has indeed been deployed.

11.2 Running Smoke Tests in the Pipeline

When deploying an application, it is important to test that the new version of the application actually works. Typically, this is done through a smoke test—a pretty simple test that nonetheless tests many aspects of the application: that the application process runs, that it binds to the port it is supposed to, and that it can answer requests. Often, this implies that both the configuration and database connection are sane as well.

When to Smoke?

Smoke tests cover a lot of ground at once. A single test might require a working network, correctly configured firewall, web server, application server, database, and so on to work. This is an advantage, because it means that it can detect many classes of errors, but it is also a disadvantage, because it means the diagnostic capabilities are low. When it fails, you don't know which component is to blame and have to investigate each failure anew.

Smoke tests are also much more expensive than unit tests. They tend to take more time to write, take longer to execute, and are more fragile in the face of configuration or data changes. So, typical advice is to have a low number of smoke tests, maybe one to 20, or maybe about 1% of the unit tests you have.

As an example, if you were to develop a flight search and recommendation engine for the Web, your unit tests would cover different scenarios that the user might encounter and that the engine produces the best possible suggestions. In smoke tests, you would just check that you

157

can enter the starting point, destination, and date of travel, and that you get a list of flight suggestions at all. If there is a membership area on that web site, you would test that you cannot access it without credentials and that you can access it after logging in. So, three smoke tests, give or take.

White Box Smoke Testing

The examples mentioned above are basically black box smoke testing, in that they don't care about the internals of the application and approach the application just like a user. This is very valuable, because, ultimately, you care about your user's experience.

Sometimes, there are aspects of the application that aren't easy to smoke test yet break often enough to warrant automated smoke tests. As an example, the application might cache responses from external services, so simply using a certain functionality is not guaranteed to exercise this particular communication channel.

A practical solution is for the application to offer some kind of self-diagnosis, such as a web page from which the application tests its own configuration for consistency, checks that all the necessary database tables exist, and that external services are reachable. A single smoke test can then call the status page and raise an error whenever the status page either is not reachable or reports an error. This is a white box smoke test.

Status pages for white box smoke tests can be reused in monitoring checks, but it is still a good idea to explicitly check them as part of the deployment process. White box smoke testing should not replace black box smoke testing, but, rather, complement it.

Sample Black Box Smoke Test

The python-matheval application offers a simple HTTP end point, so any HTTP client will do for smoke testing. Using the curl command line HTTP client, a request can look like this:

```
$ curl --silent -H "Accept: application/json" \
      --data '["+", 37, 5]' \
      -XPOST http://127.0.0.1:8800/
42
```

An easy way to check that the output matches expectations is by piping it through grep.

```
$ curl --silent -H "Accept: application/json" \
      --data '["+", 37, 5]' \
      -XPOST http://127.0.0.1:8800/ | grep ^42$
42
```

The output is the same as before, but the exit status is non-zero, if the output deviates from the expectation.

Adding Smoke Tests to the Pipeline and Rolling Releases

A naive integration of smoke tests in a delivery pipeline is to add a smoke test stage after each deployment stage (that is, one after the test deployment and one after the production deployment). This setup prevents a version of your application from reaching the production environment if it failed smoke tests in the testing environment. Because the smoke test is just a shell command that indicates failure with a non-zero exit status, adding it as a command in your deployment system is trivial.

If you have just one instance of your application running, this is the best you can do. However, if you have a farm of machines, and several instances of the application running behind some kind of load balancer, it is possible to smoke test each instance separately during an upgrade and abort the upgrade if too many instances fail the smoke test.

All big, successful tech companies guard their production systems with such partial upgrades guarded by checks, or even more elaborate versions thereof.

A simple approach to such a rolling upgrade is to extend the Ansible playbook for the deployment of each package and have it run the smoke tests for each machine before moving to the next (Listings 11-3 and 11-4).

Listing 11-3. File `smoke-tests/python-matheval`: A Simple HTTP-Based Smoke Test

```
#!/bin/bash
curl  --silent -H "Accept: application/json" \
      --data '["+", 37, 5]' -XPOST  http://$1:8800/ \
      | grep ^42$
```

Listing 11-4. File `ansible/deploy-python-matheval.yml`: A Rolling Deployment Playbook with Integrated Smoke Test

```
---
- hosts: web
  serial: 1
  max_fail_percentage: 1
  tasks:
    - apt:
        update_cache: yes
        package: python-matheval={{package_version}}
        state: present
        force: yes
    - local_action: >
        command ../smoke-tests/python-matheval
        "{{ansible_host}}"
      changed_when: False
```

As the number of smoke tests grows over time, it is not practical to cram them all into the Ansible playbook, and doing that also limits reusability. Here, they are instead in a separate file in the deployments utils repository.[1] Another option would be to build a package from the smoke tests and install them on the machine that Ansible runs on.

While it would be easy to execute the smoke tests command on the machine on which the service is installed, running it as a local action (that is, on the control host on which the Ansible playbook is started) also tests the network and firewall part and, thus, more realistically mimics the actual usage scenario.

11.3 Configuration Templates

When you have more than one software package to deploy, you build a pipeline for each one. As long as the deployment pipelines are similar enough in structure—mostly using the same packaging format and the same technology for installation—you can reuse the structure, by extracting a *template* from the first pipeline and instantiating it several times to create separate pipelines of the same structure.

If you look carefully over the pipeline XML configuration developed before, you might notice that it is not very specific to the python-matheval project. Apart from the Debian distribution and the name of the deployment playbook, everything in here can be reused for any software that's been Debian-packaged.

To make the pipeline more generic, you can define *parameters* (*params* for short) as the first thing inside your pipelines, before the <materials> section (Listing 11-5).

---

[1]https://github.com/python-ci-cd/deployment-utils.

Listing 11-5. Parameter Block for the python-matheval Pipeline, to Be Inserted Before the Materials

```
<params>
  <param name="distribution">stretch</param>
  <param name="deployment_playbook">deploy-python-matheval.yml
  </param>
</params>
```

Then replace all occurrences of stretch inside each stage's definition with the placeholder #{distribution} and deploy-python-matheval. yml with #{deployment_playbook}, which leaves you with XML snippets such as

```
<exec command="/bin/bash">
  <arg>-c</arg>
  <arg>deployment-utils/add-package \
       testing #{distribution} *.deb</arg>
</exec>
```

and

```
<exec command="/bin/bash" workingdir="deployment-utils/
ansible/">
  <arg>-c</arg>
  <arg>ansible-playbook --inventory-file=testing
     --extra-vars="package_version=$(&lt; ../../version)"
     #{deployment_playbook}</arg>
</exec>
```

The next step toward generalization is to move the stages to a *template*. This can either be done, again, by editing the XML config or in the web interface with Admin ➤ Pipelines and then clicking the Extract Template link next to the pipeline called python-matheval.

The result in the XML looks like Listing 11-6, if you chose debian-base as the template name.

Listing 11-6. GoCD Configuration for Pipeline matheval Using a Template

```
<pipelines group="deployment">
  <pipeline name="python-matheval" template="debian-base">
    <materials>
      <git url=
        "https://github.com/python-ci-cd/python-matheval.git"
        dest="source" materialName="python-matheval" />
      <git url=
        "https://github.com/python-ci-cd/deployment-utils.git"
        dest="deployment-utils"
        materialName="deployment-utils" />
    </materials>
    <params>
      <param name="distribution">stretch</param>
      <param name="deployment_playbook">deploy-python-matheval.
                  yml</param>
    </params>
  </pipeline>
</pipelines>
<templates>
  <pipeline name="debian-base">
    <!-- stages definitions go here -->
  </pipeline>
</templates>
```

Everything that's specific to this one software package is now in the pipeline definition, and the reusable parts are in the template. The sole exception is the `deployment-utils` repository, which must be added to each pipeline separately, because GoCD has no way to move a material to a template.

Adding a deployment pipeline for another application is now just a matter of specifying the URL, target (that is, name of a group in the Ansible inventory file), and distribution. You will see an example of that in the next chapter. This amounts to fewer than five minutes of work, once you're used to the tooling.

11.4 Avoiding the Rebuild Stampede

When you have a sizable number of pipelines, you'll notice an unfortunate pattern. Whenever you push a commit to the `deployment-utils` repository, it triggers the rebuild of all pipelines. That's a waste of resources and keeps the build agent or agents occupied, so building of packages based on actual source code changes gets delayed until after all the build jobs have finished.

GoCD's materials have an *ignore* filter that is meant to avoid costly rebuilds when only documentation has changed (Listing 11-7). You can use this to ignore changes to all files in the repository, thus avoiding a rebuild stampede.

Listing 11-7. GoCD Material Definition That Avoids Triggering the Pipeline

```
<git url="https://github.com/python-ci-cd/deployment-utils.git"
     dest="deployment-utils" materialName="deployment-utils">
   <filter>
       <ignore pattern="*" />
       <ignore pattern="**/*" />
   </filter>
</git>
```

The * filter matches all files in the top-level directory, and **/* all files in subdirectories.

When you change the material configuration of the `deployment-utils` material in all pipelines to have these ignore filters, a new commit to the `deployment-utils` repository does not trigger any pipelines. GoCD still polls the material and uses the newest version when starting a pipeline. As with all pipelines, the version of the material is the same at all stages.

Ignoring all the files in a repository is a blunt tool and requires you to manually trigger the pipeline for a project, to exercise changes to the deployment playbooks. So, starting from GoCD version 16.6, you can invert the filter conditions with `invertFilter="true"`, to create white lists (Listing 11-8).

Listing 11-8. Using White Lists in GoCD Materials to Selectively Trigger on Changes to Certain Files

```
<git url="https://github.com/python-ci-cd/deployment-utils.git"
        invertFilter="true" dest="deployment-utils"
        materialName="deployment-utils">
  <filter>
    <ignore pattern="ansible/deploy-python-matheval.yml" />
  </filter>
/git>
```

Such a white list configuration per pipeline causes commits to the `deployment-utils` repository to trigger only the pipelines that the changes are relevant for.

11.5 Summary

When you configure your pipelines to deploy exactly the same version that has been built in the same instance of the pipeline, you can use this to install old versions or conduct rollbacks.

Pipeline templates allow you to extract the commonalities between pipelines and maintain those only once. Parameters bring in the variety needed to support diverse software packages.

CHAPTER 12

Security

What's the impact of automated deployment on the security of your applications and infrastructure? It turns out there are both security advantages and things to be wary of.

12.1 The Dangers of Centralization

In a deployment pipeline, the machine that controls the deployment must have access to the target machines where the software is deployed. In the simplest case, there is a private SSH key on the deployment machine, and the target machines grant access to the owner of that key.

This is an obvious risk, because an attacker gaining access to the deployment machine (the GoCD agent or the GoCD server controlling the agent) can use this key to connect to all the target machines, gaining full control over them.

Some possible mitigations include the following:

- Implement a hardened setup of the deployment machine (for example, with SELinux or grsecurity).

- Password-protect the SSH key and supply the password through the same channel that triggers the deployment, such as through an encrypted variable from the GoCD server.

© Moritz Lenz 2019
M. Lenz, *Python Continuous Integration and Delivery*,
https://doi.org/10.1007/978-1-4842-4281-0_12

- Use a hardware token for storing SSH deployments keys. Hardware tokens can be safe against software-based key extraction.

- Have separate deployment and build hosts. Build hosts tend to require far more software installed, which exposes a bigger attack surface.

- You can also have separate deployment machines for each environment, with separate credentials.

- On the target machines, allow only unprivileged access through said SSH key and use something like sudo, to allow only certain privileged operations.

Each of these mitigations has its own costs and weaknesses. To illustrate this point, note that password-protecting SSH keys helps if the attacker only manages to obtain a copy of the file system, but not if the attacker gains root privileges on the machine and, thus, can obtain a memory dump that includes the decrypted SSH key.

A hardware-based storage of secrets provides good protection against keys' theft, but it makes use of virtual systems harder and must be purchased and configured.

The sudo approach is very effective at limiting the spread of an attack, but it requires extensive configuration on the target machine, and you need a secure way to deploy that. So, you run into a chicken-and-egg problem that involves some extra effort.

On the flip side, if you don't have a delivery pipeline, deployments have to occur manually. So, now you have the same problem of having to give humans access to the target machines. Most organizations offer some kind of secured machine on which the operator's SSH keys are stored, and you face the same risk with that machine as the deployment machine.

12.2 Time to Market for Security Fixes

Compared to manual deployments, even a relatively slow deployment pipeline is still quite fast. When a vulnerability is identified, this quick and automated rollout process can make a big difference in reducing the time until the fix is deployed.

Equally important is the fact that a clunky manual release process seduces the operators into taking shortcuts around security fixes, thus skipping some steps of the quality-assurance process. When that process is automated and fast, it is easier to adhere to the process than to skip it, so it will actually be carried out even in stressful situations.

12.3 Audits and Software Bill of Materials

A good deployment pipeline tracks when which version of a software package was built and deployed. This allows one to answer questions such as "How long did we have this security hole?", "How soon after the issue was reported was the vulnerability patched in production?", and maybe even "Who approved the change that introduced the vulnerability?"

If you also use configuration management based on files that are stored in a version control system, you can answer these questions even for configuration, not just for software versions.

In short, the deployment pipeline provides enough data for an audit.

Some legislation requires you to record a software bill of materials[1] in some contexts, for example, for medical device software. This is a record of the components contained in your software, such as a list of libraries and their versions. While this is important for assessing the impact of a

---

[1]Wikipedia, "Software bill of materials," https://en.wikipedia.org/wiki/Software_bill_of_materials, 2018.

license violation, it is also important for figuring out which applications are affected by a vulnerability in a particular version of a library.

A 2015 report by HP Security found that 44% of the investigated breaches were made possible by vulnerabilities that have been known (and presumably patched) for at least two years. This, in turn, means that you can nearly halve your security risk by tracking which software version you use where, subscribe to a newsletter or feed of known vulnerabilities, and rebuild and redeploy your software with patched versions on a regular basis.

A continuous delivery system doesn't automatically create such a software bill of materials for you, but it gives you a place where you can plug in a system that does.

12.4 Summary

Continuous delivery provides the ability to react quickly and predictably to newly discovered vulnerabilities. At the same time, the deployment pipeline itself is an attack surface, which, if not properly secured, can be an attractive target for an intruder.

Finally, the deployment pipeline can help you to collect data that can offer insight into the use of software with known vulnerabilities, allowing you to be thorough when patching these security holes.

CHAPTER 13

State Management

Continuous delivery (CD) is nice and easy for a stateless application, that is, for an application that does not have data persistently stored. Installing a new application version is a simple task, which just requires the installation of the new binaries (or sources, in case of a language that's not compiled), stopping the old instance, and starting a new instance.

As soon as there is persistent state to consider, things become more complicated. Here, I will consider traditional relational databases with schemas. You can avoid some problems by using a schema-less "noSQL" database, but you don't always have that luxury. If you do go schema-less, you have to deal with older data structures inside the application code, not through the deployment process.

Along with the schema changes, you might have to consider data migrations, which might involve such things as filling out missing values with a default or importing data from a different data source. In general, such data migrations fit the same pattern as schema migrations, which is to execute either a piece of SQL and data definition language (DDL)[1] or run an external command that directly talks to the database.

---

[1]Wikipedia, "Data definition language," https://en.wikipedia.org/wiki/Data_definition_language, 2018.

© Moritz Lenz 2019
M. Lenz, *Python Continuous Integration and Delivery*,
https://doi.org/10.1007/978-1-4842-4281-0_13

171

13.1 Synchronization Between Code and Database Versions

State management is difficult, because code is usually tied to a version of the database schema. There are several cases in which this can cause problems.

- Database changes are often slower than application updates. If version 1 of your application can only deal with version 1 of the schema, and version 2 of the application can only deal with version 2 of the schema, you have to stop version 1 of the application, do the database upgrade, and start up version 2 of the application only after the database migration has finished.

- Rollbacks to a previous version of an application, and thus its database schema version, become painful. Typically, either a database change or its rollback can lose data, so you cannot easily do an automated release and rollback over these boundaries.

To elaborate on the last point, consider the case in which a column is added to a table in the database. In this case, the rollback of the change (deleting the column again) loses data. Conversely, if the original change is to delete a column, that step usually cannot be reversed. You can re-create a column of the same type, but the data is lost. Even if you archive the deleted column data, new rows might have been added to the table, and there is no archived data for these new rows.

13.2 Decoupling Application and Database Versions

There is tooling that can help you get your database schema into a defined state reproducibly, but it does not solve the problem of potential data loss through rollbacks for you. The only practical approach is to establish collaboration between the application developers and the database administrators and break up problematic changes into multiple steps.

Suppose your desired change is to drop a column that has a NOT NULL constraint. Simply dropping the column in one step comes with the problems outlined in the previous section. Instead, you might be able to do the following steps:

1. Deploy an application version that can deal with reading NULL values from the column, even though NULL values are not yet allowed.

2. Wait until you're sure you don't want to roll back to an application value that cannot deal with NULL values.

3. Deploy a database change that makes the column nullable (or give it a default value).

4. Wait until you're sure you don't want to roll back to a schema version where this column is NOT NULL.

5. Deploy a new version of the application that doesn't use the column anymore.

6. Wait until you're sure you don't want to roll back to a version of your application that uses this column.

7. Deploy a database change that drops the column entirely.

Some scenarios allow you to skip some of these steps or fold multiple steps into one. Adding a column to a table is a similar process, as follows:

1. Deploy a database change that adds the new column with a default value (or allows NULL values).

2. Deploy a version of the application that writes to the new column.

3. Optionally run some migrations that fill the column for old rows.

4. Optionally deploy a database change that adds constraints (like NOT NULL) that weren't possible at the start.

   … with the appropriate waits between the steps.

Example of a Schema Change

Suppose you have a web application backed by a PostgreSQL database and, currently, the application logs login attempts into the database. So, the schema looks like this:

```
CREATE TABLE users (
    id          SERIAL,
    email       VARCHAR NOT NULL,
    PRIMARY KEY(id)
);

CREATE TABLE login_attempts (
    id          SERIAL,
    user_id     INTEGER NOT NULL REFERENCES users (id),
    success     BOOLEAN NOT NULL,
    timestamp   TIMESTAMP NOT NULL DEFAULT NOW(),
    source_ip   VARCHAR NOT NULL,
    PRIMARY KEY(id)
);
```

As the load on the web application increases, you realize that you are creating unnecessary write load for the database and start logging to an external log service. The only thing you really require in the database is the date and time of the last successful login (which your CEO insists you show on each login, because an auditor was convinced it would improve security).

So, the schema you want to end up with is this:

```
CREATE TABLE users (
    id          SERIAL,
    email       VARCHAR NOT NULL,
    last_login  TIMESTAMP NOT NULL,
    PRIMARY KEY(id)
);
```

A direct database change script to get there would be

```
DROP TABLE login_attempts;
```

```
ALTER TABLE users
    ADD COLUMN last_login TIMESTAMP NOT NULL;
```

but that suffers from the problem previously outlined that it ties the schema version to the application version, but also that you cannot introduce a NOT NULL column without a default and without supplying values for it.

Let's break it down into separate steps that don't suffer from these problems.

Creating the New Column, NULLable

The first step is to add the new column, users.last_login, as optional (by allowing NULL values). If the starting point was version 1 of the schema, this is version 2:

```
CREATE TABLE users (
    id           SERIAL,
    email        VARCHAR NOT NULL,
    last_login   TIMESTAMP,
    PRIMARY KEY(id)
);
```

-- table login_attempts omitted, because it's unchanged.

Running apgdiff, Another PostgreSQL Diff Tool,[2] against the two scheme files gives us:

```
$ apgdiff schma-1.sql schema-2.sql
```

```
ALTER TABLE users
    ADD COLUMN last_login TIMESTAMP;
```

which is the forward migration script from schema 1 to schema 2. Note that we don't necessarily need a rollback script, because every application version that can deal with version 1 of the schema can also deal with schema version 2 (unless the application does something stupid like SELECT * FROM users and expects a certain number or order of results. I'll assume the application isn't that stupid).

This migration script can be applied to the database while the web application is running, without any downtime.

---

 i   MySQL has the unfortunate property that schema changes are not transactional and they lock the whole table during the schema changes, which negates some advantages you gain from incremental database updates.

---

[2]www.apgdiff.com/.

To mitigate this, there are some external tools that work around this by creating a modified copy of the table, gradually copying the data from the old to the new table, then finally doing a rename to replace the old table. One such tool is gh-ost[3] by GitHub.

These tools typically come with only limited support for foreign key constraints, so evaluate them carefully before using them.

When the schema change has finished, you can deploy a new version of the web application that writes to users.last_login whenever a successful login occurs. Note that this application version must be able to deal with reading NULL values from this column, for example, by falling back to table login_attempts, to determine the last login attempt.

This application version can also stop inserting new entries into table login_attempts. A more conservative approach is to defer that step for a while, so that you can safely roll back to an older application version.

Data Migration

In the end, users.last_login is meant to be NOT NULL, so you have to generate values for where it's NULL. Here, table last_login is a source for such data.

```
UPDATE users
  SET last_login = (
        SELECT login_attempts.timestamp
          FROM login_attempts
         WHERE login_attempts.user_id = users.id
```

---

[3]https://github.com/github/gh-ost/.

```
        AND login_attempts.success
    ORDER BY login_attempts.timestamp DESC
        LIMIT 1
    )
WHERE users.last_login IS NULL;
```

If NULL values remain, say, because a user never logged in successfully, or because table last_login doesn't go back far enough, you must have some fallback, which could be a fixed value. Here, I'm taking the easy road and simply using NOW() as the fallback.

```
UPDATE users SET last_login = NOW() WHERE last_login IS NULL;
```

These two updates can again run in the background, while the application is running. After this update, no further NULL values should show up in users.last_login. After waiting a few days, and verifying that this is indeed the case, it's time to apply the necessary constraint.

Applying Constraints, Cleaning Up

Once you are confident that there are no rows that miss values in the column last_login, and that you aren't going to roll back to an application version that introduces missing values, you can deploy an application version that stops using table login_attempts, dispose of the table login_attempts, and then apply the NOT NULL constraint (see also Figure 13-1).

```
DROP TABLE login_attempts;

ALTER TABLE users
    ALTER COLUMN last_login SET NOT NULL;
```

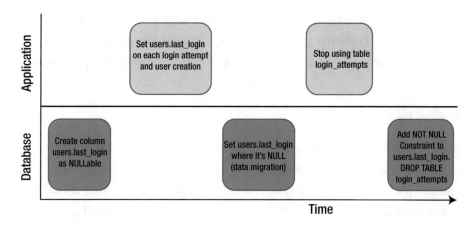

Figure 13-1. *Sequence of application and database update steps. Each database version is compatible with the application versions before and after it, and vice versa.*

In summary, a single logical database change has been spread over three database updates (two schema updates and one data migration) and two application updates.

This makes application development a bit more of an effort, but you gain operational advantages. One of these advantages is keeping the application releasable to production at all times.

Prerequisites

If you deploy a single logical database change in several steps, you must do several deployments, instead of one big deployment that introduces both code and schema changes at once. That's only practical if the deployments are (at least mostly) automated, and if the organization offers enough continuity that you can actually finish the change process.

If the developers are constantly putting out fires, chances are they never get around to adding that final desired NOT NULL constraint, and some undiscovered bug will lead to missing information later down the road.

You should also set up some kind of issue tracker with which you can trace the path of schema migrations, to make sure that none remains unfinished, for example, in the case of a developer leaving the company.

Tooling

Unfortunately, I know of no tooling that fully supports the intertwined database and application release cycle that I outlined. There are tools that manage schema changes in general. For example, Sqitch[4] and Flyway[5] are rather general frameworks for managing database changes and rollbacks.

On the lower level, there are tools such as apgdiff that compare the old and new schemas and use that comparison to generate DDL statements that bring you from one version to the next. Such automatically generated DDLs can form the basis of the upgrade scripts that Sqitch or Flyway then manage.

Some ORMs also come with frameworks that promise to manage schema migrations for you. Carefully evaluate whether they allow rollbacks without losing data.

Structure

If you decouple application deployments from schema deployments, it follows that you must have at least two separately deployable packages: one for the application and one for the database schema and schema migration scripts. If you want or have to support rollbacks of database schemas, you must remember that you need the metadata associated with the new schema to be able to roll back to the old version.

---

[4]https://sqitch.org/.
[5]https://flywaydb.org/.

The database description for version 5 of the schema doesn't know how to roll back from version 6 to version 5, because it knows nothing about version 6. So, you should always keep the newest version of the schema file package installed and separate the installed version from the currently active database version. The tooling that controls the schema migrations can be independent of the application and its schema, and so should live in a third software package.

No Silver Bullet

There is no single solution that manages all your data migrations automatically for you during your deployments. You have to carefully engineer the application and database changes to decouple and deploy them separately. This is typically more work on the application development side, but it buys you the ability to deploy and roll back without being blocked by database changes.

Tooling is available for some pieces but typically not for the big picture. Someone has to keep track of the application and schema versions—or automate them.

13.3 Summary

State held in a database can complicate application upgrades.

Incompatible data structure and schema changes can be broken up into several smaller steps, each of which is compatible with the previous one.

This allows application upgrades without downtime, at the cost of having to do several application and schema deployments.

CHAPTER 14

Conclusions and Outlook

After reading this book, you should have a solid understanding of how and why to implement continuous integration (CI) and continuous delivery (CD) for a Python project. It is not a small undertaking, but the many examples should get you started pretty quickly, and even an implementation of only some aspects can give you benefits. In a collaborative environment, showing these benefits makes it easier to convince others that it's worth spending your time on toolchain and process improvements.

14.1 What's Next?

In this final chapter, let's look at some concepts that can help you grow an even more mature software development process that ties into CI and CD.

Improved Quality Assurance

Improving the quality of your software can be as simple as increasing the unit test coverage of your application. However, not all classes of errors can be caught that way, for example, performance regressions or errors for cases you didn't think of before.

© Moritz Lenz 2019
M. Lenz, *Python Continuous Integration and Delivery*,
https://doi.org/10.1007/978-1-4842-4281-0_14

CHAPTER 14 CONCLUSIONS AND OUTLOOK

To catch performance regressions, you can create a separate performance testing environment and run a predefined set of load and performance tests in this environment. You can add this as another stage to your deployment pipeline.

Handling unexpected cases is harder, because, by definition, they catch you by surprise. For certain types of applications, automatic fuzzing can find inputs that make your application crash and provide these inputs as examples to the developers.

There are architectural approaches to make your applications robust against unexpected user input and error scenarios, but from a tooling perspective, the best you can do is to make the application's reactions to such errors more robust.

Specialized error trackers can help you to identify such errors. They give developers more insight into how to reproduce and diagnose those errors. For example, Sentry[1] is an open source, centralized error tracker with a hosted solution available.

Metrics

In bigger systems and organizations, gathering and aggregating metrics is a requirement for keeping the system manageable. There is even a trend to base monitoring on time-series data.

In the context of a deployment system, some data points you can collect include the start date and duration of each stage or task, which version it built, and the characteristics of that particular version, including performance data, usage data such as engagement rates, size of the generated artifacts, defects and vulnerabilities discovered, and so on.

---

[1]https://getsentry.com/welcome/.

Making sense of the gathered data is not always easy, and entire books have been written about it. Nonetheless, it's a good idea to establish a way to collect metrics of all kinds and to create dashboards that help interpret them.

Infrastructure Automation

Configuration management is essential for scaling your infrastructure, but a tool such as Ansible alone isn't enough for all needs and scales.

Configuration in a Database, Secrets Management

As the amount of configuration data grows, keeping it in plain text files becomes impractical. Therefore, you will have to maintain a database of the configuration and use Ansible's *dynamic inventory* mechanism[2] to propagate the data into the configuration management system.

However, storing passwords, private keys, and other secrets in a database is always a delicate business. You need an application on top of the database, to avoid leaking such secrets to users who shouldn't have access to them.

Such applications already exist. Dedicated secret management systems store secrets in encrypted form and carefully control access to them. Examples of such applications are Keywhiz,[3] by Square, or Vault,[4] by HashiCorp, the authors of Vagrant.

Secret management systems typically offer plug-ins to create service accounts, such as MySQL or PostgreSQL database accounts, and rotate their passwords without human involvement. Crucially, it also means that no human has to ever see the randomly generated passwords.

---

[2]http://docs.ansible.com/ansible/developing_inventory.html.
[3]https://square.github.io/keywhiz/.
[4]www.hashicorp.com/blog/vault.html.

Instead of pushing application configuration into the machines or containers where the application runs, you can also build your applications to fetch the configuration from a central location. Such a central location is typically called a *service discovery* system. Tools such as etcd,[5] from the CoreOS project, and Consul,[6] from HashiCorp, make it easier to manage large amounts of configuration. They also provide additional features, such as basic monitoring for services and exposing only working instances of a service end point to consumers.

To illustrate, consider that an application requiring large amounts of configuration data could be supplied with just a secret key for authentication against the service discovery system and the information about which environment it runs in. The application then reads all of its other configuration from the central service. If the application needs access to a storage service, and there are multiple instances that can provide this service, the monitoring service makes sure that the application gets the address of a working instance.

Such a service discovery approach allows a pattern called *immutable infrastructure*. This means you build a container (such as a Docker container or even a virtual machine image) once, then, instead of propagating just your application through the various testing environments, you propagate the whole container through them. The cluster management system provides the credentials for connecting to the service discovery system; otherwise, the containers remain unchanged.

Infrastructure As Code

A traditional CD system, as described in the earlier chapters, is usually limited to one branch in a source control system, because there is only one testing environment for deploying the code.

---

[5]https://github.com/coreos/etcd.
[6]www.consul.io/.

Cloud infrastructure changes the game. It allows declarative descriptions of whole environments, consisting of several databases, services, and virtual servers. Instantiating a new environment then becomes a matter of executing a single command, allowing you to deploy each branch into a new, separate environment.

Leading tools for creating new environments are Terraform[7] and CloudFormation.[8]

14.2 Conclusions

Automating deployments makes both software development and operation more efficient and more pleasant. I've shown you a gentle and practical introduction to it, and, in turn, enabled you to introduce CD to your organization.

This is a big step for an organization that develops software, but it is also a small part of automating your infrastructure and a small part of the journey to an efficient and resilient software development process.

---

[7]www.terraform.io/.

[8]https://aws.amazon.com/cloudformation/.

Index

A

Ansible, 87
    application-specific module, 95
    apt module, 93
    apt_repository and
        apt_key modules, 97
    connections and
        inventory, 88–90
    copy module, 91
    deployment, 104–105
    file module, 93
    modules, 90
    package module, 94
    playbooks, 95–98
    shell module, 90
    template module, 92
    yum and zypper module, 94
Ansible playbook fragment, 154
Ansible playbook,
    GoCD configuration, 155
Ant/Rake builds, 124
apgdiff tool, 180
Application programming
    interface (API), 4
Application-specific module, 95
Apt module, 93–94
Automated testing
    catastrophic failures, 2

debugging aid, 3
design aid, 3–4
downsides, characteristics, 7
feedback, 1–2
product specification, 4

B

Building packages
    debian repositories (*see* Debian
        packaging, dh-virtualenv)
    Python source tarball, 67–68

C

Config references, 134
Connection method, 88–90
Continuous delivery (CD),
    171, 183, 186
    Debian package,
        installation, 64–65
    debian repositories, 63–64
    GoCD, 66
    pipeline architecture, 59–61
    testing environment, 61–62
Continuous integration (CI),
    39, 40, 53, 183
Copy module, 91

© Moritz Lenz 2019
M. Lenz, *Python Continuous Integration and Delivery*,
https://doi.org/10.1007/978-1-4842-4281-0

Printed in the United States
By Bookmasters